COMPEL

Copyright

Dedication

This book is dedicated to my precious wife Patti and my son Isaiah. God has truly blessed me with His best! Thank you for your support, prayers and encouragement in this faith-filled journey. Without you, this book would not have become a reality. I love you with all of my heart. Thank you for believing in the dream.

Acknowledgements

My deepest appreciation to my senior pastors Art and Kuna Sepúlveda. You have been my spiritual parents from the very beginning of my walk with the Lord. I wouldn't be the person I am today if you hadn't taken the time to obediently answer the call and speak into my life. Words alone cannot express my deep gratitude, thank you.

A special thanks to Sharla Nunes for her talent in editing; to Rachel Brownlow Lund, for your excellence in the copy edit and proofreading; and to my sister in law Raquel Pacheco for creating the logo and book cover. Thank you.

Contents

Foreword

Pastor Wally Matanza challenges me in ways that few authors ever do. Lots of people have something to say, but few people will stand by the words and genuinely live by conviction of what they have said. *"Compel"* contains words that convict, inspire, ignite and will cause you to take a welcomed second look... which is a healthy thing for any Christian desiring to follow Christ without compromise.

"Compel" lives up to the authentic, character-driven, passionate and enthusiastic trademark that will awaken any longing heart in their pursuit for Christ. The challenge that *"Compel"* will have on your life will be both encouraging and motivating. The simple yet profound and deep-reaching impact of *"Compel"* – that will breathe life into any Christian – can be summed up as "revolutionary."

Without compromise, *"Compel"* reveals what the missing link is in multitudes of Christians' hearts today – a burning desire to fulfill the greatest Gospel vision revealed from the heart of the Father to His church: The Great Commission.

I am honored and privileged to call Pastor Wally Matanza a spiritual son. His love for Jesus Christ is without question; his love for people is without compromise; and his pursuit of following Jesus' mandate to "compel people from the highways and byways that His Father's house may be filled" is genuine and passionate. Yet, the work of the Holy Spirit in his life, as with the church of Jesus Christ, no man can take credit for but God Himself. His labor of love for lost, dying, crying and sighing humanity is infectious, inspiring and compelling.

It's been said that the destiny of the church is not a mystery. It's a decision. And you are one decision away from a totally different life after reading this book. Enjoy the journey. Let the Holy Spirit speak and stir within you. Truly, God is calling His church to live a "compelling life" that will draw all to know Him. The church's life is a letter, a living epistle to be known and read by all.

"Compel" without question will draw you closer to Him with everything in you!

Pastor Art Sepúlveda
Word of Life Christian Center
Honolulu, HI

Foreword

Compel will awaken every believer to be bold and committed ambassadors for Christ. This book will strengthen men and women of God to understand their call to their generation. It will inspire them to reach out to others with the same compassion that Jesus reached out to them with. As healing and transformation was brought to their lives, so too will they want to bring that to others as they read through this book.

Wally Matanza is one of my spiritual sons, whose testimony in his book will captivate every child of God to want to let God work through their life. As Wally prayed, walked by faith and yielded to the Holy Spirit, he saw the hand of God touch and change people's lives. They were healed, delivered and set free! They experienced miracles because one ordinary man was willing to step out for someone else.

As an individual opens their heart with every chapter, they will be compelled and motivated to be who God needs them to be for a dying and hurting world, and God will mightily pour through them to bring about breakthrough!

I believe you will be blessed by this book.

Pastor Kuna Sepúlveda
Word of Life Christian Center
Honolulu, HI

Introduction

I have endeavored to break this book into manageable sections that are supported with real-life testimonies. We will take everything one step at a time and help you to become that bold witness God has always intended you to be. I want to encourage you to take your time in meditating on each chapter and allow the Word to incubate your faith.

The world as we know it today is very bold in its sinful lifestyle. We see it in our neighborhood, our community and the media. We need to be that much bolder if we, as the body of Christ, are to be a voice in our generation. Be Bold as a Lion and allow your true nature in Christ to awaken as you step out and obey by faith!

It is my hope and prayer that this book would bring you encouragement and help you to develop greater confidence as a witness for Jesus. There is a boldness within you that awakens the moment you step out in faith to be a witness for Christ.

When you encounter God's love for you, it will compel you to reach others around you.

Chapter 1

COMPEL

"For the love of Christ compels us, because we judge thus: that if One died for all, then all died; and He died for all, that those who live should live no longer for themselves, but for Him Who died for them and rose again."

2 Corinthians 5:14-15 NKJV

Like many people who grew up in religious families, I was raised with a deep sense of religiosity but a weak relationship with God. I attended church every Sunday, and even served as an altar boy while in elementary school. There was no shortage of religious routine, but I would not say that I personally had a relationship with Christ.

That all changed back in 1997 when I became an absolute mess due to a break up with my then-girlfriend. I had broken her trust through my infidelity, and she was completely unwilling to work it out. To make matters worse, she ended up dating my roommate several weeks later! The breakup was heart-rending, and I found myself haunted by vain imaginations that seemed too overwhelming to overcome. That was when I cried out to God for help, and He rescued me from one of my darkest hours.

When you fully experience God's love for you, it will compel you to reach others around you. Ever since I surrendered my life to God, I have had many opportunities to share the gospel with others. Now, introducing people to Jesus Christ has become one of my great passions in life.

****

I first sensed my calling into full-time ministry in 1999, when I was stationed in Kaneohe, Hawaii serving in the United States Marine Corps. By that time, I'd read the bible from cover to cover several times over and would often find myself in tears as I read God's word. It was as if the scriptures leaped off the pages and came to life in me.

Experiencing God's tangible presence and goodness in my life had changed me forever, and I felt a stirring in my heart to see my entire family come to the saving knowledge of Christ. My Christmas leave from the military was coming up, so I decided to engage in a 21-day commitment to prayer and fasting, to prepare myself spiritually for the immense task I felt called toward: witnessing to my family.

When I arrived in San Diego, my cousins wondered why I was so skinny. Since I was just learning about the power of prayer and fasting myself, I let the subject drop; I didn't think they would understand if I tried to explain.

One day, my uncle had some pain in his foot, so I asked him if I could pray for him.

"Sure," he said, leaning back to observe as I placed my hands on his feet. I don't think anyone had ever offered to pray for his healing before; nonetheless, he was very receptive.

The moment I finished praying, he beamed at me, a huge smile plastered to his face.

"Wow, the pain is gone!" exclaimed my uncle. "You know what, Wally Boy, we should have a bible study tonight. Then you can share with everybody!"

This experience was the first time I had ever prayed for anyone in pain. I was simply applying what I had learned according to the Word. It was a step of faith, and God confirmed His word. My uncle offered his home to conduct a bible study, and I was beyond excited. It was the open door of opportunity that I had been praying for.

That night, my uncle's house was filled with family and friends ready to hear the gospel. I was so nervous because public speaking had never been one of my strengths in high school. But for the sake of their salvation, I was willing to do whatever needed to be done. I did not have it all figured out beforehand, but I prayed that their hearts would be open, and that the Lord would give me the very words to share.

"But how can they believe in Him if they have never heard about Him? And how can they hear about Him unless someone tells them" (Romans 10:14 NLT).

That night the house was so packed that some people were sitting on the floor throughout the house, while others stood in the kitchen. I preached my first sermon, and everyone prayed the sinner's prayer. We even had a healing line for those who needed prayer for their physical bodies.

It was a powerful time of ministry, and those who were dear to my heart were there to receive. Everyone present either received Christ into their hearts for the first time or rededicated their lives to live for the Lord. In another room, I prayed for those who wanted to receive the baptism of the Holy Spirit and they all began to pray in other tongues.

The Holy Spirit filled me, and I was compelled to bathe my friends and family in prayer. I believe the Lord wants to accomplish this kind of miracle with your family and friends. All He is looking for is your willingness and obedience.

Jesus gave His followers the most compelling vision ever when he said, "Go into all the world and preach the gospel to every creature. He who believes and is baptized will be saved; but he who does not believe will be condemned" (Mark 16:15-16 NKJV).

The salvation of humanity hinged upon the obedience of the early disciples. They were to spread the good news regarding the Savior of the world! Their responsibility was to communicate the greatest message of hope in all of history!

Today, this responsibility and wonderful privilege lies on each and every one of us who believe in Jesus. Through Christ, anyone who believes can receive mercy and forgiveness.

Jesus paid the ultimate price for the penalty of our sin. The gospel is simple: Believe that Jesus is the Son of God who came to take away the sin of the world, and you shall be saved and inherit eternal life in heaven.

One of the most zealous disciples who followed Jesus was known in the bible as the Apostle Paul. He faced many challenges and adversities, beyond what many have the capacity to endure mentally and physically. But because of his undeniable love for the Lord, he persevered and became a mighty vessel for God.

The Apostle Paul said, "...I have been in prison more often, been whipped times without number, and faced death again and again. Five different times the Jewish leaders gave me thirty-nine lashes. Three times I was beaten with rods. Once I was stoned. Three times I was shipwrecked. Once I spent a whole night and a day adrift at sea. I have traveled on many long journeys. I have faced danger from my own people, the Jews, as well as from the Gentiles. I have faced danger in the cities, in the deserts, and on the seas. And I have faced danger from men who claim to be believers but are not. I have worked hard and long, enduring many sleepless nights. I have been hungry and thirsty and have often gone without food. I have shivered in the cold, without enough clothing to keep me warm. Then, besides all this, I have the daily burden of my concern for all the churches" (2 Corinthians 11:23-28 NLT).

What motivated Paul to endure such suffering for the cause of Christ? What moved him to spread the good news of salvation regardless of personal sacrifice? What propelled him to invest his life for the purposes of God? To keep moving forward in the face of persecution, even to the point where his own life was at stake?

The answer? It was Paul's unwavering love for Christ that compelled him to live for God.

The Apostle Paul's commitment and zeal to serve the Lord has been so inspiring for me. The moment he gave his heart to God, his entire life was centered on the purposes of Jesus. He burned with passion to see the lost saved. It was Christ's overwhelming love that moved him to forsake his own personal pursuits and instead live solely for the glory of God.

Before Paul served the Lord, he persecuted those who believed in Jesus and threw them in prison. When he realized the magnitude of his sin, it absolutely broke him to a place of repentance. God in his mercy gave Paul a new heart and a fresh start, and Paul lived his new life to the fullest!

****

"There is no other name under heaven given among men by which we must be saved" (Acts 4:12 NKJV).

It's only through the name of Jesus that a person can obtain salvation and forgiveness from their past. Anyone who calls upon that name shall be saved. There is power in the name of Jesus to blot out every sin you have committed. Through your faith in Christ, you become a partaker of God's divine nature.

There are people who have been deceived to think that they have to earn their way to heaven through good works, but that is not the case. In fact, it's much simpler than that: through faith alone, you can be saved!

"For by grace you have been saved through faith, and that not of yourselves; it is the gift of God" (Ephesians 2:8 NKJV).

This is good news! You don't have to earn your way to heaven. God has already made provision for us through His Son Jesus Christ. We can simply receive it by faith that what Jesus Christ did on the cross was sufficient for our redemption and forgiveness. This is the gospel that people need to hear.

****

The first time I heard the good news was back in 1995. I was a senior in high school, living a life that wasn't pleasing to God. I was constantly fighting, cutting class, getting high with my friends, and headed the wrong way fast. Realizing that I was floundering, my cousin Marlon invited me to a bible study.

To be honest, bible study was the last thing on my mind during that season of my life. The only things that concerned me were girls, partying, and having a great time. I had no vision, and no direction. I was just living life one day at a time.

"What am I going to do there?" I remember asking him.

Then he said something that caught my interest: "Well, there are a lot of pretty girls there... and they have good food, too."

"Girls?" With that, I agreed to attend.

For the next several weeks I became a big distraction to that gathering, interrupting and flirting with the girls while the minister talked. I'd do drugs before bible study and then devour the food at the meeting. As if the situation wasn't bad enough, I invited all of my friends along with me as well. (Fortunately, and though I probably didn't deserve it, the minister was very patient with me throughout my many interruptions.)

Then, something changed. One night, I looked at everybody's faces and noticed how seriously engaged they were with the sermon. Curious, I decided to listen to what the minister was saying.

After a few minutes, I began to feel like God himself was speaking directly to me. I will never forget one scripture the minister shared that night: "God demonstrates His own love toward us, in that while we were still sinners, Christ died for us" (Romans 5:8 NKJV).

That scripture exploded in my heart. I knew the many sins I had committed, and knowing that Jesus had taken on the punishment that my sins deserved broke up the hardness of my heart. It is that unconditional love that compels me to be a witness for Jesus today.

As the minister went on to share his own personal experience, the presence of God and His goodness began to touch my heart. At that point, I didn't understand what that feeling was, but I knew I was experiencing something powerful. Looking back, that was the very first time I heard the good news of the Lord Jesus Christ.

In Luke 15:7, the Bible states that "there will be more joy in heaven over one sinner who repents than over ninety nine just persons who have no need of repentance." In other words, heaven is filled with joy each time we lead others to the saving knowledge of Jesus Christ.

My cousin may not have been the one to share the message of salvation with me personally, but he compelled me to come to the bible study where I could hear about the love of God. Even though I did not surrender my life to God that day, a significant seed of God's love was planted in my heart.

"I planted the seed in your hearts, and Apollos watered it, but it was God who made it grow" (1 Corinthians 3:6-8 NLT).

The seed is the word of God. Each time we share God's love with others, we are sowing seed into their hearts. Then, another person may come along and water that seed through prayer or a word of encouragement. Both are working together for a common goal, and that is to eventually lead that person to a personal relationship with Christ.

It's not important who does the planting, or who does the watering. One is not more important than the other because both are necessary. What's important is that God makes the seed grow. Only He can touch our hearts through our obedience. And so, both the planter and the waterer work together with the same purpose in mind, and both will be rewarded for their own hard work.

****

Back in high school, I was heavily involved in gangs. As a result, I got kicked out of several schools and had to register in different school districts.

The last high school I attended in southern California just happened to be where many of my rival gangs attended school. I remember sitting in class together with them, knowing they were plotting an attack against me because of the gang I represented.

Finally, the day came where about 15 guys jumped me. For nearly two minutes they surrounded me and swung fists at my face as I desperately tried to defend myself. Eventually, school security broke it up.

My gang involvement progressed to even worse incidents, until my mother decided to send me to northern California to live with my grandparents.

Away from all the negative influences, my grades—and my life—finally began taking a turn for the better. I graduated from high school and landed a stable job as a butcher at the local supermarket.

Despite my situational improvements, I couldn't shake the feeling that my life lacked purpose or direction.

"Is this all there is to life?" I thought one day, as I wrapped a cut of pork and handed it to a customer.

Seeking to fill the void, I enlisted in the Marine Corps. I figured if I was going to join the military, I was going to join the toughest branch of them all (at least in my opinion).

Fortunately, the three months of boot camp helped to mold my character and leadership. After my combat training, my staff sergeant at our station in Honolulu, Hawaii invited me to attend Word of Life Christian Center. And that is where I fully surrendered my heart to Jesus.

For the first time in my life, I really began to understand that all of heaven takes notice and celebrates whenever a sinner repents and turns from his evil ways. Regardless of the things that I have done in life, Jesus loves me unconditionally.

Today, when I share my testimony with others who did not know me previously, they have difficulty believing my past. I guess it's because I have completely changed how I carry myself. I used to take offense with that until the Lord spoke to my heart and said, "Wally, you should be thankful that I have so transformed your life, that people can no longer tell the life you once lived."

God is in the business of transforming people's lives, and He can do the same for you. Even as you are reading this book, change is beginning to take place in your heart. As you apply what you learn in this book, people will no longer be able to tell how intimidated you used to be to witness or share your faith with others. Your true nature in Christ is to be bold as a lion, inspiring others to share Jesus with the world!

So what would it take for you to share your faith with others? What is hindering you and holding you back? Take an honest personal inventory of where you are in your witness for Christ. When was the last time you shared God's unconditional love with your family or with your neighbors? There are so many people who are desperate for God.

****

Once, I heard a missionary share about the work her ministry was doing in Thailand. I was so inspired that I decided to go on a mission trip and partner with them. Upon arriving in Thailand, I began to grasp the extent of human trafficking and how many children fell prey to it.

In America, it's easy to judge these circumstances and wonder how they could have arisen; but in Thailand, where millions of people live below the national poverty line, the tale is quite common. It goes something like this: Traffickers go into remote, poverty stricken villages and promise the world to the parents. They say things like, "Look at the living conditions of your child. You can't even provide a decent meal. If you allow us to take the child with us, we will take good care of them and make sure they get a proper education." Many times parents have the best intentions for their children, but if they cannot see any other way out of their poverty, they may sign the documents and send off their children. To them it's a hopeless situation either way. What they don't realize is that, by signing the papers, they just entrusted their child to a human trafficker.

Picture a little girl who is now in the custody of strangers. She is brought into an underground market and thrown into the center of a dark room where people begin bidding for her as if she were livestock. Feelings of abandonment and rejection wash over her, a sense of loneliness and hopelessness overwhelming her.

Then a man walks across the market place while the bidding is in progress, and he sees the girl crying. Moved with compassion, he strides toward the slave trader and inquires, "How much for the little girl?"

Upon hearing the price, he pays the auctioneer in full. Then he approaches the girl and hands her the bill of sale telling her, "Daughter, you are free." As the man heads home, the little girl chases after him, joyful tears streaming down her face. "My Redeemer, My Redeemer!" she shouts, loud enough for everyone to hear. "Please" she says to the man, "let me go along with you and serve you."

We were all like that child at one point in our life. We were, each of us, a slave of sin in need of a Savior. Jesus came along and rescued us from darkness. He delivered us from the death grip of the enemy out of His love and compassion for us. Now that we have obtained freedom in Christ, how will you respond to your Redeemer, Jesus?

I pray that your heart would cry out to the Lord out of gratitude and say, "My life belongs to you, God. May your love and compassion burn in me so that I, too, may serve you as a minister of the gospel. I am compelled by your love to reach out to others who are weighed down by hopelessness and imprisoned by sin. Lead me and guide me to those who are crying out to you."

Jesus gives us this parable regarding the Great Supper:

"A certain man gave a great supper and invited many, and sent his servant at supper time to say to those who were invited, "Come, for all things are now ready." But they all with one accord began to make excuses. The first said to him, "I have bought a piece of ground, and I must go and see it. I ask you to have me excused." And another said, "I have bought five yoke of oxen, and I am going to test them. I ask you to have me excused." Still another said, "I have married a wife, and therefore I cannot come." So the servant came and reported these things to his master. Then the master of the house, being angry said to his servant, "Go out quickly into the streets and lanes of the city, and bring in here the poor and the maimed and the lame and the blind. And the servant said, "Master, it is done as you commanded, and still there is room." Then the master said to the servant, "Go out into the highways and hedges, and compel them to come in, that my house may be filled" (Luke 14:16-23 NKJV).

Compel is about the driving force behind why we do what we do as witnesses for Christ. It's about the unconditional love and compassion of Jesus that was demonstrated for us at the cross-- the same love that compels us to share about Christ with others.

Jesus said that we are to "Compel people to come in, that His house may be filled." Take the love and compassion of Jesus Christ that has been richly poured out into your heart and share it with the world. The love of God deposited in you is so great that it cannot be contained; it must be dispensed into the lives of those around you. As long as you are willing to take the first step of obedience, God will give you the courage to share your faith and touch people's lives.

Prayer:

"Father, I recognize that it is the love of Christ that compels me to share my testimony with others. I am thankful for the love and sacrifice that you demonstrated for me at the cross and for the forgiveness of my sin. May that always be the reason why I serve you all the days of my life. I do not want to do things out of religious routine or out of obligation. I choose to serve you wholeheartedly, compelled by your love to share with the world about your unconditional love for them. In Jesus' name. Amen."

The moment you step out in faith, there is a boldness within you that awakens.

Chapter 2

BOLD AS A LION

The wicked flee when no one pursues,
But the righteous are bold as a lion.
Proverbs 28:1 NKJV

When my son was four years old, I watched a movie with him called "Madagascar." The story follows Alex the Lion, a popular show lion that entertains all the people who visit the zoo. Each day, to the crowd's delight, Alex would run around the cage wildly and let out a mighty roar. Then, at the end of everyday, he'd get pampered by the zookeepers and groomed to perfection for the next day's show. Since Alex the Lion is a show lion, he never had to hunt for his own food. Instead, the zookeepers ensure that he's well taken care of, providing him with a luxurious personal dwelling and the finest steaks available to him on demand.

The plot thickens when, during the course of the movie, Alex the Lion and his friends are mistakenly transported out to the wild. While in transit to the San Diego Zoo, the cargo that they were contained in was accidentally knocked off the ship. After a couple of days of surviving without food, Alex starts to visualize everyone around him as a piece of steak—including his best friend Marty the Zebra!

Because this lifestyle is so far out of his comfort zone, Alex the Lion does not know what to do. He is in a foreign environment with no daily food supply; meanwhile, all he can think about is his next meal!

Eventually, the hunger pangs he experiences create a stirring within him that causes his true nature to bubble to the surface! The natural instincts of the predator inside of him are no longer dormant; they have awakened!

Similarly, there is a boldness within many Christians that lies dormant but can be awakened in Christ Jesus. As a Christian, your spiritual instincts must be awakened in order for you to discover the true nature you possess. When you step out of your comfort zone, there will be a stirring of faith and boldness in your spirit, and your true nature in Christ will come forth!

Unfortunately, many believers today have reduced their Christianity into something that can be likened to that of a show lion at the zoo. There are hundreds of thousands of professing Christians who attend church on a regular basis and even serve in the ministry, but they have yet to experience the joy of witnessing to others about who Jesus is in their lives.

Many battle with fear of rejection, intimidation, and feelings of inadequacy, and because they do not know how to overcome these, they choose to opt out of sharing their faith. Sharing your faith in Christ is one of the most joyful and fulfilling experiences that has been entrusted to us as a believer. Have you ever wondered about the lives of people that you can impact through your obedience?

I remember back in 2001, a friend called and cried out for help. It was during my third day of prayer and fasting. I usually set aside these times as a source of spiritual strengthening in my faith and relationship with God. My friend shared with me that a relative of his was experiencing demonic manifestations, and her family had become very worried about her. A man's voice was coming out of her, and she was not in her right mind at all.

At this point in my walk with the Lord, I had never encountered anyone who was completely possessed by evil spirits. Nevertheless, I told my friend that I would visit this woman right away. To bolster my resolve, I brought along another friend of mine—a classmate from bible school.

When we arrived at the woman's house that evening, my heart felt like it was going to explode from nervousness. This was uncharted territory for me in my Christian walk, and way out of my comfort zone. It took an enormous amount of willpower to cast out thoughts like, "If this spirit manifests, I'm either going to punch this woman out or run for my life!"

Fortunately, I was reminded of the wise words Jesus said.

"Behold, I give you the authority to trample on serpents and scorpions, and over all the power of the enemy, and nothing shall by any means hurt you" (Luke 10:19 NKJV).

Remembering those words, I snapped out of it and rebuked that spirit of fear!

As I entered the house, every hair on my body stood up. The entire family had gathered together, and I could sense a strong demonic presence in our midst. It was as if these demon spirits did not want me there and were actively trying to intimidate me through fear.

I sat down in front of the possessed woman and introduced myself, even though she had her eyes closed. As soon as she opened her eyes and looked into mine, her eyes got really big and she started to scream violently at me.

At that moment, something awakened inside of me, and I experienced a boldness I had never known before. Without thinking about the situation, I found myself leaping over the coffee table and grabbing hold of her head. Overcome by the Holy Spirit, I turned my focus to the demon inside of her.

"Come out in Jesus' Name!" I commanded the demon.

The woman immediately fainted right there in the living room!

Around me, the family members who were present started crying; they did not understand what had just taken place. I instructed my friend to continue commanding the remaining spirits to come out; and while he was praying over her, I used the opportunity to witness to the woman's family.

By the end of the night, the entire family surrendered their hearts to Christ, including the woman that I had prayed for. When you step out in faith, God will always show up!

One of the greatest obstacles people need to face in order to be a Bold witness for Christ is to get out of their comfort zone! People are so accustomed to their daily routines that they hesitate to do something new, especially if it involves the possibility of being rejected. We all desire to walk worthy of the calling and be well pleasing to God, but many times we just don't know where to begin.

At the close of 2010, we had a congregation member (whom I will refer to as Mary) who decided to participate in a short-term mission trip to Tondo, one of the poorest and most underdeveloped districts in Manila Philippines.

A week before we were scheduled to depart, Mary began having second thoughts about going. She shared that she had never left the country and had always been intimidated about witnessing to others. Her parents were also worried about her going and had asked for contact numbers in case of an emergency. In response, I encouraged her to be confident and be at peace, and that God was going with her on this mission trip.

When the team arrived in Manila Philippines, we met with the church leaders who we were partnering with and had a short orientation meeting. Our first outreach took place in Tondo, one of the most densely populated areas in the world. In a span of only 9 miles, more than 407,000 people lived in slums and poverty.

Before we journeyed into the community, I had assembled a drama team to assist in helping us attract attention to our cause. When we arrived in Tondo, I sent out four men dressed in all black with long-sleeve shirts and white-painted faces to walk the streets. The spectacle attracted a lot of people, and they soon started following our oddly dressed drama team to see what was going on.

It had rained the day before so the roads were very muddy. Eventually, however, we found a large gathering area with dry ground—a perfect spot for our presentation. As we opened up our outreach with our drama presentation, hundreds of people started to gather in the street. It was literally the crossroads of that community, but with permission, we stopped all incoming traffic and preached right in the middle of the road. People surrounded us, many of them lined up along the railing of the second-floor balcony.

After we captured their attention, we preached the message of salvation, healing and deliverance, and about 350 people surrendered their hearts to Jesus Christ. Then our team laid hands on the sick and the diseased, and they saw the power of God manifest. It was a glorious sight to see!

By the way, guess who was in the mix of everything taking place? Remember timid Mary? In the midst of a great crowd, she was laying hands on the sick! In a place considered to be one of the most dangerous places in the Philippines, she became Bold as a Lion! Her faith to be a bold witness was awakened and stirred as she stepped out of her comfort zone and placed her absolute trust in God to minister through her.

Are you like Mary? Do you have a desire to share your faith with others, but because of fear, intimidation, or lack of knowledge, you hesitate to speak out and ultimately become paralyzed in your witness?

The good news is that there is hope for you! If Mary can break through and become as Bold as a Lion, so can you! The same Jesus who transformed and equipped her to be a bold and effective minister of the gospel is the same Jesus who will empower you!

Mary's Testimony
"Thank you Wally for allowing me to be a part of the great mission team. The experience will burn and live in my heart forever. It was amazing to see 12 of us at different places in our walk with God, but we all had the same heart, to save souls. I will never forget my first mission trip. It has burned a mark upon my heart that I will never forget. This experience has changed and transformed my life."

****

During Christmastime, one of my co-workers blessed my son Isaiah with a Lego train collection that he had been building for many years. Though building the collection had been a longtime hobby of his, he decided to pass the Legos to my son as a gift.

With a grateful heart, I took home a big box filled with a classic Lego train and pirate ship set and wrapped it for my son to open on Christmas Eve. I'll never forget the joy that lit up his face when he opened them!

That week we unpacked the Lego collection, and there must have been 2,000 pieces! It was exciting for us, but the only drawback was there were no instructions on how to build it. My son and I worked away on it, but it felt as if we were not getting anywhere.

After a couple of hours trying to figure it all out, I started organizing everything piece by piece according to the shape of each building block. It made finding the piece we needed a lot easier.

Being a bold witness for Christ can be overwhelming at first, especially when you don't know where to begin. Many Christians do not have a blueprint on how to confidently and effectively share the message of salvation with their family, friends and loved ones.

When I discovered the reality of heaven and hell through the Word of God, the urgency to minister to my family was overwhelming. After all, if there is anyone we would want to see saved, shouldn't it be the people we care about the most?

Book of Revelation portrays a vivid picture of the reality of heaven and hell: "And I saw the dead, small and great standing before God, and books were opened. And another book was opened which is the Book of Life. And the dead were judged according to their works, by the things which were written in the books. The sea gave up the dead who were in it, and Death and Hades delivered up the dead who were in them. And they were judged, each one according to his works. Then Death and Hades were cast into the lake of fire. This is the second death.

And anyone not found written in the Book of Life was cast into the lake of fire"(Revelation 20:12-15 NKJV).

Are the names of your loved ones written in the Book of Life? Don't miss out on the opportunity to reach them. Hell was never meant to be anyone's eternal destiny. It is an everlasting fire prepared for the devil and his angels.

We are all going to have to stand before Christ to be judged one day. Therefore we should work hard to persuade others to turn away from their sinful life and turn to Jesus for forgiveness. God loved us so much that He made a way for us all to be saved. Let's seize every opportunity that we have to be the bold witness that God has called us to be.

I once had the privilege of ministering to a millionaire couple who I met in the Philippines through a mutual friend. I could have been intimidated if I kept my eyes on my own ability because I had no business knowledge. Instead, I thought to myself, "When will I have another opportunity like this?"

The couple and I—along with our mutual friend—met for breakfast and had some great time of fellowship. The man shared with my friend and I about his business and his upcoming projects. I asked if we could pray a blessing over his family and his business, and he was very open. Afterwards, I asked him and his wife how they were doing on their spiritual journey.

"We are very busy with work and do not have time for church. But we do many good deeds, and we are always giving to the poor," they replied. "We have several big projects coming up as you can see, and it's going to bring in a lot of revenue."

This was the moment of truth. I was either going to back down or continue to witness. Then the wisdom of the Holy Ghost came upon me.

"I think it's great that your business is flourishing and that you are doing many good deeds," I said. "But the word of God tells us, 'What profit is it to a man if he gains the whole world, and is himself destroyed or lost' (Luke 9:25). "It also says that 'All our righteousness in our own strength is like filthy rags in the sight of God' (Isaiah 64:6). God is a jealous God and He wants to have preeminence in our lives. 'Jesus is the Way, the Truth, and the Life, and no one comes to the Father except through Him' (John 14:6)."

At that, the couple bowed their heads, and I extended the invitation to them to surrender their lives to God and receive Jesus as their personal Savior. They were ready with open hearts. God touched that wonderful couple as we prayed.

Had I not stepped out of my comfort zone and obeyed God, that couple would not have received Christ into their heart. And if their lives were to expire without Jesus, they would not be able to spend eternity in heaven with God our Maker, the lover of our soul. Regardless of what a person's success may be, one thing is for sure, we all need Jesus as our Savior.

As a Christian, it is our responsibility to share this message with the world around us, no matter who they are. Say this prayer as you get started in your faith journey on becoming Bold as a Lion.

Prayer:

"Father, I open my heart to receive from you through reading this book. I know that you are not willing that anyone should perish. It is my heart's desire to see the lost saved, especially my loved ones. I yield myself to you Holy Spirit to be your mouthpiece that you can speak through. Now, Lord grant to Your servant that with all boldness I may speak Your Word. Stretch out Your hand to heal. I pray that signs and wonders may be done through the name of Your holy Servant Jesus. Amen."

No matter what mistakes you have made, God has orchestrated a master plan for your life.

Chapter 3

MASTER PLAN

"... I'll show up and take care of you as I promised and bring you back home. I know what I am doing. I have it all planned out - plans to take care of you, not abandon you, plans to give you the future you hope for."

Jeremiah 29:10-11 MSG

No matter what mistakes you have made, God has orchestrated a master plan for you to fulfill your purpose. Many people get stuck in the lowest points of their lives because they do not understand or know of God's unconditional love for them. Some can't see past their shortcomings, especially in their battle against sin. They think because they are not perfect, they are automatically disqualified. But grace is God giving us what we did not deserve. It is His unmerited favor.

So let us take a journey and look at the beauty of God's grace in the life of a son who, by many reasons, did not deserve to be loved and forgiven. However, it was because of grace that his father loved him anyway. This is the story of the Prodigal son:

"A man had two sons, when the younger told his father 'I want my share of your estate now instead of waiting until you die.' His father agreed to divide his wealth between his sons.

A few days later this younger son packed all of his belongings and took a trip to a distant land and wasted all his money on parties and prostitutes. About the time his money was gone, a great famine swept over the land and he began to starve. He persuaded a local farmer to hire him to feed his pigs. The boy became so hungry that even the pods he was feeding the swine looked good to him, and no one gave him anything.

When he finally came to his senses he said to himself, "at home, even the hired men have food enough to spare and here I am dying of hunger." I will go home to my father and say, "father, I have sinned against both heaven and you and am no longer worthy of being called your son. Please take me on as a hired man."

So he returned home to his father and while he was still a long distance away his father saw him coming and was filled with compassion, ran towards him, embraced him and kissed him. His son said to him "father, I have sinned against heaven and you and am no longer worthy to be called your son." But the father said to his servant, "bring out the best robe and put it on him, and put a ring on his hand and sandals on his feet. Bring the fatted calf and kill it and let us eat and be merry. For this son of mine was dead and has returned to life. He was lost and is found." So the party began.

Meanwhile, the older son was in the field working. When he returned home, he heard dance music coming from the house and so he asked one of the servants what was going on and they said "your brother's back, and your father has killed the calf we were fattening and has prepared a great feast to celebrate his coming home again, unharmed."

The older brother was angry and wouldn't go in. His father came out and begged him. But he replied, "all these years I have worked hard, and never once refused to do a single thing you told me to. And in all that time you never gave me one young goat for a feast with my friends. Yet when this son of yours comes back after spending your money on prostitutes, you celebrate by killing the finest calf we have on the place." The father said, "You and I are very close and everything I have is yours. But it is right to celebrate. For he is your brother, and he was dead and has come back to life. He was lost and is found" (Luke 15:11-32 TLB).

The Prodigal son's father embraced his younger son with love and forgiveness. This is a great metaphor for God's love towards each and every one of us.

Many people have different opinions and labels about you because of your past mistakes. You may even have a label for yourself. Who do you listen to? Whom do you believe?

It doesn't matter what people think or say about you. People will always have their opinions. What matters most is what God says about you.

The Prodigal son's older brother felt the complete opposite of his father. He knew about his brother's faults and sins. He even communicated his reasoning against his father's celebration for his brother. He justified that in all his years of serving his father, not once had he received such a celebration even though he had always been obedient. He further pointed out that his brother had spent all his money on wild living. Why should he be getting such a wonderful homecoming after such a disgraceful lifestyle?

Grace, God's unmerited favor, is a gift, kindness, favor and blessing. We don't deserve God's grace, but He freely bestows it upon us when we honor him with our faith.

As for the Prodigal son, his living resulted in him downsizing his true self-image. At one point, he even told himself he was no longer worthy of being called a son and would be more than happy to accept the role of a servant in his father's house. He felt so guilty for the wrong he had done. His self-image was distorted by the lies of the enemy, and sin.

"We must warn each other every day, while it is still today that none of us will be deceived by sin and hardened against God" (Hebrews 3:13 NLT).

The heart is hardened through the deceitfulness of sin. When people participate in sin—whether it be lying, stealing, drinking, fornicating, partying or something else—it may be enjoyable for a period of time, but they do not realize that it ultimately affects their self-image. Through sin, they begin to drift away from God's master plan for their lives.

Sin opens the doors to other sin, and before you know it, nothing satisfies you. You begin to take on a low self-esteem, asking questions like, "How did I get here?" and giving answers like, "This is not who I am."

When the Prodigal son hits an all-time low in his life, he finally comes to his senses and runs back to his father. He thought his father would be upset and disappointed in him. He was willing to humble himself, ask for forgiveness and be a servant in his father's house. Instead, when his father saw him coming home from a distance, he ran towards his son filled with love and compassion.

God the Father, the Father of all fathers, is your spiritual dad. He is waiting for you to run to Him, just like the Prodigal son ran to his father. God your Father is waiting for you, and He will embrace you just as you are, despite everything you have done in your past.

There comes a time in our lives when we realize that the seductions of the world never satisfy. We begin to question, "Is this what life is really about? What is my purpose? Why am I here?"

Know that God has a master plan for your life. You have a specific purpose that you were destined to fulfill. You were not an accident.

When people are without God, they are in a state of brokenness, hurt, hopelessness, and this was never part of His Master Plan. His Master Plan is to heal and restore you. The mercy of God forgives us completely of all of our past shortcomings, failures and mistakes. The grace of God reinstates us to our true identity and restores our value according to God's original design for our life.

Remember what the father said to his servants regarding the Prodigal son: "Bring out the best robes and put it on him." In the story, the robes represent righteousness, a right standing with God. Nothing has changed regarding the father's relationship with his son. Then the father said, "put a ring on his finger," which represents authority. The first thing the father does is to help his son grasp his true identity not as a servant, but as a son.

The depth of your understanding regarding your identity as a child of God hinges upon your relationship with God— not based on your talents, abilities, job, works or performance, but based on your faith about who God says you are. You are God's precious son or daughter, you are righteous, victorious, prosperous, healed, and more than a conqueror!

****

"Yet in all these things we are more than conquerors through Him Who loved us. For I am persuaded that neither death nor life, nor angels nor principalities nor powers, nor things present nor things to come, nor height nor depth, nor any other created thing, shall be able to separate us from the love of God which is in Christ Jesus our Lord" (Romans 8:37-39 NKJV).

Before the Apostle Paul came to know the Lord, he murdered Christians. But when he encountered Jesus on the road to Damascus, his life was dramatically changed. He became one of the most passionate and zealous followers of Christ! He reached more people and covered more territory than any of the other 12 apostles. When he discovered God's mercy and grace over his life, he was absolutely persuaded that there was nothing in this world that could sever his relationship with God.

No matter how far you run, God always has open arms ready to embrace you coming back home. Understand that there is nothing you could possibly do to make God love you any more. And there is nothing that you can do to make God love you any less. God's love for you is unconditional.

Before I received Christ, my mindset was that I needed to get better before I was to even set foot in the church. I didn't understand that the gospel was not based on my works but by my faith in what Jesus had done for me on the cross.

As mentioned earlier, I joined the United States Marine Corps and was stationed in Hawaii. After experiencing a painful breakup, my heart longed to find a church. I prayed to the Lord that if He could remove the pain in my heart, I would serve Him all the days of my life. It was time for me to start taking steps in getting my life right with God.

That's when my staff sergeant invited me to Word of Life Christian Center in Honolulu. It was there that I was recaptured by God's unconditional love, and I gained a full understanding of His mercy upon my life. It was at this local church that I discovered God's ultimate plan for my life and began to realize that despite my past, He had a master plan to get me where I needed to be.

Under the mentorship and spiritual guidance of Pastors Art and Kuna Sepúlveda, who I consider to be my spiritual parents, vision awakened within me, and I chose to leave behind the tumultuous life I'd once lived once and for all.

"You shall know the truth, and the truth shall set you free" (John 8:32 NKJV).

If you desire to know God's plan for your life, start by finding a local church where you can grow spiritually in your relationship with God. Begin by asking Him to forgive you of all your faults and shortcomings, and receive His forgiveness by faith.

God will give you a fresh start and empower you to live your life to your fullest potential. It will be one of the most rewarding decisions of your life and will absolutely change the course of your destiny.

I want to encourage you to get yourself a bible and start seeking the Lord by reading His word. Find a local church and a mentor who can help speak into your life, someone who is willing to coach you along the way through life's toughest challenges.

For inspiration on your journey, take a look at the following Psalm: "God, You are my God; early will I seek You; my soul thirsts for You; my flesh longs for You in a dry and thirsty land where there is no water. So I have looked for You in the sanctuary, to see Your power and Your glory. Because Your loving kindness is better than life, My lips shall praise You. Thus I will bless You while I live; I will lift up my hands in Your name. My soul shall be satisfied as with marrow and fatness, and my mouth shall praise You with joyful lips" (Psalm 63:1-5 NKJV).

For those of you who already have a relationship with God, ask yourself, "How am I doing in my devotional life?" Are you in constant communication with God, or have you allowed weeks or months to go by without spending quality time with the Lord in prayer?

Understand that when your vertical relationship with God is strong, it will have a significant impact in your horizontal relationship with people. When you are constantly spending quality time with God in unbroken fellowship, you begin to take on some of His character and unconditional love. You become a dispenser of that which is deposited in your own spirit. For example, when strife attempts to come against your marriage, it's easy to forgive quickly and completely. When you understand the power of God's forgiveness, it will change you. "Freely you have received, freely you shall give." (Matthew 10:8 NKJV)

"Therefore the kingdom of heaven is like a certain king who wanted to settle accounts with his servants. And when he had begun to settle accounts, one was brought to him who owed him ten thousand talents. But as he was not able to pay, his master commanded that he be sold, with his wife and children and all that he had, and that payment be made. The servant therefore fell down before him, saying, 'Master, have patience with me, and I will pay you all.' Then the master of that servant was moved with compassion, released him, and forgave him the debt. "But that servant went out and found one of his fellow servants who owed him a hundred denarii; and he laid hands on him and took him by the throat, saying, 'Pay me what you owe!'

So his fellow servant fell down at his feet and begged him, saying, 'Have patience with me, and I will pay you all.' And he would not, but went and threw him into prison till he should pay the debt. So when his fellow servants saw what had been done, they were very grieved, and came and told their master all that had been done. Then his master, after he had called him, said to him, 'You wicked servant! I forgave you all that debt because you begged me. Should you not also have had compassion on your fellow servant, just as I had pity on you?' And his master was angry, and delivered him to the torturers until he should pay all that was due to him. "So My heavenly Father also will do to you if each of you, from his heart, does not forgive his brother his trespasses" (Matthew 18:23-35).

He who is forgiven much, loves much. When you know where you came from and you never forget what the Lord has forgiven you of, it will be reflected in the way you live your life for Him. It will not be a burden for you to serve the Lord and forgive others.

So why is it that under the banner of grace, people tend to do less for the Lord? The Apostle Paul said to the Corinthian church that "by the grace of God I am what I am, and His grace toward me was not in vain; but I labored more abundantly than they all, yet not I, but the grace of God which was with me" (1 Corinthians 15:10 NKJV).

The Apostle Paul used to persecute believers before his conversion on the road to Damascus. But when he encountered the goodness of God, he turned from his wicked ways and surrendered his life to Jesus Christ. He felt that it was his reasonable service to serve the Lord in preaching the gospel and believed that God's divine empowerment to do so upon his life was not in vain. Paul was so grateful for what the Lord had done for him that there were no arguments whatsoever.

"But know this, that in the last days perilous times will come: for men will be lovers of themselves, lovers of money, boasters, proud, blasphemers, disobedient to parents, unthankful, unholy, unloving, unforgiving, slanderers, without self-control, brutal, despisers of good, traitors, headstrong, haughty, lovers of pleasure rather than lovers of God, having a form of godliness but denying its power. And from such people turn away (2 Timothy 3:1-5 NKJV).

This passage reminds me of a story about a public auction on an old violin. Though the auctioneer didn't feel the violin was worth the effort of attempting to sell it, he held up the musical instrument with a smile and began the auction.

"Who will start the bid for this old violin?" he asked.

No one seemed interested. They paid no attention to the auctioneer for what seemed to be a very long period of time. However, right before the auctioneer was about to conclude the bidding, an old grey haired man stepped forward, blew the dust off the instrument and fine tuned the strings. Then he picked up the bow and began to play a heavenly melody.

Once the old man finished playing, he handed the violin back to the auctioneer to resume the bidding.

"Who will bid for this old violin?" the auctioneer asked again.

This time, as the auctioneer held up the bow, someone from the audience yelled out, "one thousand dollars!" Another said, "two thousand dollars!" And yet another called out, "three thousand dollars!"

In the end, the old violin was sold for a significant price. The people clapped and cheered.

"What changed the worth of the violin?" an audience member asked the auctioneer. "One moment, hardly anyone was interested. A few moments later, it sold for a large amount."

The auctioneer replied, "It was the touch of the Master's hand."

That story was based on a poem shared by the renowned poetess Myra Welsh who, in 1950, went on to be with the Lord. In Welsh's poem, the master's touch revealed the potential of what that old violin could do. It just needed some fine-tuning in the hands of the master.

No matter what mistakes you've made, God has a master plan orchestrated for you to fulfill your purpose. He wants to reawaken what has, perhaps, been dormant in you for some time.

The gifts and callings of God are irrevocable. Your shortcomings and past mistakes in life do not change that. You may believe you have lowered your self worth, but God wants to remind you that He loves you unconditionally and has a great plan and purpose for your life. If you would but believe in the God who strongly believes in you, your life can be radically different. The Master, Jesus, will bring forth a beautiful sound from your life that will bring glory to His name when you surrender all to Him.

As in the poem, what was once discarded and rejected became a great instrument when placed in the Master's hand. You don't have to downsize your dream. God has a bright future for your life! You serve a mighty God Who is always for you and never against you.

I'm not sure what challenges you are facing today, but I know that there is hope for you. Truly, with God, nothing is impossible. You can live a great life with unlimited potential if you devote yourself to your Maker, Almighty God, and allow Him to breathe life back into your soul.

The grace of God on your life is not in vain. You are God's answer to a generation in desperate need of hope. It's the love of Christ that compels us to be the voice that God needs us to be to the world. If you are ready for His Master Plan for your life, pray this prayer...

Prayer:

"Father, I believe You have a master plan for my life. I ask you to forgive me for entertaining doubt and unbelief at times. I am fully persuaded that when I surrender my life in the hands of the Master, I will fulfill my God-given potential and purpose in life. I choose to keep you at the center of my heart. Lead and guide me into your perfect will, Lord. In Jesus' name. Amen."

One act of compassion can change the world.

Chapter 4

COMPASSION

And when she opened it, she saw the child, and behold, the baby wept. So she had compassion on him, and said, "This is one of the Hebrews' children."

Exodus 2:6 NKJV

I started attending bible school in 1999, immediately after I finished my term in the Marine Corps. I was so hungry to learn more about God and His plan for my life. I participated in the intercessory prayer with a handful of bible students, and we prayed for different nations after class. We also went to Waikiki and ministered to tourists.

After some time, I started to develop a desire to share the gospel abroad. I wasn't sure exactly how that was going to happen, so I decided to take a step of faith and purchase a passport. Knowing that James 2:26 NKJV says, "faith without works is dead," I started to act upon what I believed God had placed in my heart to do.

In 2011, our church participated in a mission trip to Thailand. We quickly realized how rampant human trafficking was there. Children from between the ages of 3 to 18 are caught up in this dark world. They feel abandoned. Usually, their parents or relatives sell them into human slavery because of poverty. Some of these children, both boys and girls, are raped 40 times a day, sexually violated by men from different countries.

These children have no choice. There are layers upon layers of bitterness, hurt, un-forgiveness and rejection bottled up in their hearts. How do you make things better in this child's life? How do you bring back hope into their broken lives? The best thing to do is give them Jesus. Jesus is the only one who can bring total healing and restoration.

As I'm writing this, Thailand's population is estimated at 67 million people with less than one percent who identify themselves as Christian. Because so few people in Thailand know Jesus, witnesses shine as a bright light when they speak His name. That is what our mission team had the privilege of doing when we partnered with the Zoe Orphanage in Chiang Mai.

On that trip, we had the opportunity to visit remote villages and share Christ. We interacted with some of the rescued children. I remembered one of the little girls held on to one of our missionaries for the longest time, just hugging her. The little girl was so thankful that a person would go there to visit her, encourage her, love her, and bless her. I've never seen anyone hold on to somebody for that long.

Here is a testimony of one of our church members who participated in our Thailand Mission Trip:

Carly's Testimony

"I had the opportunity to go to Thailand. This was my first mission trip in another country. It was amazing, and the best experience I've ever had. Talk about the compassion of God in rescuing a generation! We went to an orphanage. What the volunteers and missionaries are doing at the Zoe Orphanage is amazing. Our mission team had the honor and privilege of working with the children at the orphanage. Many of these children were either rescued from human trafficking, or they were beggars on the streets. Each orphan had no parents or relatives who could care for them. We spent quality time and ministered to these kids.

The pastors we partnered with talked about compassion. It wasn't just a message they preached but a life that they lived. They worked closely with a rescue team, and they weren't afraid to get in the mess and rescue these children from unimaginable situations. We had a lot of opportunities to be around them and get to know the kids. In our interactions with them, there was no sign of hurt and pain from being exposed to human trafficking and/or not having their parents. They were so filled with love, joy and hope because of God's love and healing power. The people at Zoe have truly made a dramatic difference in the lives of these children. Not only are they rescuing them, but they educate and nurture them with the love and compassion that only comes from God. To witness the result of someone's compassion caused my heart to enlarge for people."

Never underestimate the power of love. One act of compassion can change the world. That is what Pharaoh's daughter witnessed when she took Moses in to be her own son.

Then the daughter of Pharaoh came down to bathe at the river. And her maidens walked along the riverside; and when she saw the ark among the reeds, she sent her maid to get it. And when she opened it, she saw the child, and behold, the baby wept. So she had compassion on him, and said, "this is one of the Hebrews' children." Then his sister said to Pharaoh's daughter, "shall I go and call a nurse for you from the Hebrew women, that she may nurse the child for you?" And Pharaoh's daughter said to her, "Go." So the maiden went and called the child's mother. Then Pharaoh's daughter said to her, "take this child away and nurse him for me, and I will give you your wages." So the woman took the child and nursed him. And the child grew, and she brought him to Pharaoh's daughter, and he became her son. So she called his name Moses, saying, "because I drew him out of the water"(Exodus 2:5-10 NKJV).

During the time this story takes place, the Israelites had multiplied so prolifically that they began to fill Egypt, and the Egyptians began to see them as a threat. The Egyptians were concerned because the Israelites greatly outnumbered them, so Pharaoh passed a law to enslave the children of Israel.

To control the Israelites, Pharaoh put slave drivers over them and placed heavy burdens over their lives, forcibly making the Israelites slaves to Pharaoh. Pharaoh became so consumed with fear that he even commanded the midwives to kill any sons born to the Hebrew women so that they could stop the Israelites from multiplying. It was during this time that Moses was born.

If you have ever watched the Ten Commandments or read about Moses in the book of Exodus, you have a mental picture of what their lives were like. Moses was a mighty man of faith. He loved to pray and have communion with God. The bible tells us it was through God's servant Moses that He brought about a great deliverance to the children of Israel who were in bondage in Egypt. We know the mighty miracles that took place through this man of God and how the Red Sea was split open. We see how the miracles that God performed through Moses literally broke the death-grip of Egypt over the children of Israel.

However, through all of that, one person who we seem to overlook is the Pharaoh's daughter. When Moses was born, slavery was rampant over the children of Israel, and Israelites were born as slaves to the Egyptians.

But then there was divine intervention over Moses' life. Pharaoh's daughter was so moved with compassion that she rescued the Hebrew child and named him Moses. What Pharaoh's daughter did not know was that she would become a significant part of God's plan to deliver the children of Israel from bondage. She had no idea that her single act of compassion would result in the deliverance of an entire nation. She did not even know God, yet she became an intricate part of God's plan and contributed greatly in the Hebrews' deliverance.

When she first encountered baby Moses, whose life was in danger because of his race, the New Living Translation Bible says that it touched her heart. Perhaps it was because she knew the helpless child had been sentenced to death. Maybe she was moved by Moses' mother's sacrifice to do whatever it took to save her child, even if it meant that she would be separated from him.

Whatever the cause, that moment touched Pharaoh's daughter's heart with such compassion that she decided to do something about the child's life. Her act of compassion changed the very course of history. It rescued Moses from his sentence of death, provided him with a home, and prepared him for his destiny!

God's plan for that generation was accomplished through compassion. And today, in our generation, God's plan is going to be accomplished through His compassion abiding inside of you.

Who would have guessed that just that one act of compassion, over one child, would change everything? Pharaoh's daughter did not know she was literally ushering in a move of God that would set the captives free from bondage. She was just simply showing compassion toward a lost child. Be a minister and dispenser of God's unconditional love. One act of compassion can change someone's life, and it truly has the potential of changing the world.

****

Recently, while checking social media, I came across a disturbing surveillance video from China that showed a two-year old girl roaming around a dark, narrow alley by herself. The alley was just wide enough for small vehicles to pass through. As this little baby toddled right in the middle of the alley, the inevitable happened: a van hit her on the head. It stopped momentarily, but only to run over her with the right side of the vehicle.

Seriously injured, the girl dropped to the ground, wallowing in the middle of the alley. Over the next few minutes, a total of nineteen people passed right by her but did nothing. One man walked by and did not even glance at the baby. Another man on a motorcycle slowed down, looked at the injured baby, and just kept going.

Finally, a garbage collector saw the child. After looking around for the little girl's guardians, she picked up the injured baby and laid her on the side of the alley. She wasn't exactly sure what happened, only that the child was seriously hurt. Eventually, the compassionate garbage collector found the girl's mother, but by then it was too late to save the little girl. The child died.

The video only lasts a few minutes, but anyone who sees it begins to wonder, "Why did so many people pass by this injured baby and not make an effort to help? Was the cause of getting involved in this injured child's life just too much?"

We can speculate. Maybe, they were simply caught up in the busyness of their own lives. Maybe they had to run an errand. However, whatever the reason, it seems obvious that they lacked compassion in the chamber of their heart.

In other circumstances, the child could have potentially accomplished much and contributed greatly to society. She could have grown up to become a Moses in her generation if someone had intervened on her behalf during that critical moment of her life.

God has a plan and a purpose for every human being born into this world. But there is an enemy called the devil that is out to "steal, kill and destroy." The enemy is doing as much as he can to hinder God's plan for your life. When good people choose to turn a deaf ear and a blind eye, evil prevails. But when you bring the light of the gospel into a dark world, there will be change and transformation.

Keep God's vision for your life at the forefront. Do not allow the enemy to steal your divine destiny in life. God's compassion in you is too great to be kept within. It must be unleashed into another dimension of faith. There is a generation waiting on the other side of your obedience. Where are you investing your energy, your time and your effort today? You must grasp what you were born to do and act upon it!

"For I know that thoughts that I think toward you, says the Lord, thoughts of peace and not of evil, to give you a future and a hope" (Jeremiah 29:11 NKJV).

Are you willing to do whatever it takes to make a difference in your generation? Is that passion on the inside of you? God is looking for people who will answer the call to reach out to those who are without Him, those without hope in this world. Humanity is in desperate need of Jesus.

At some point in our lives, we all have passed by people who were crying or dying on the inside. Perhaps these people have lost hope and fallen into a state of depression; perhaps they have deep emotional wounds they simply cannot recover from.

According to Luke 4:18 NKJV, "Jesus came to heal the brokenhearted." In Jesus they can receive healing both physically and emotionally.

Unfortunately, God's people have made too many excuses. We have too many "buts." But I am too busy. But I have an important appointment. But I am too young. But I am too old. But I am too shy. But I don't feel qualified. While we reason ourselves out of doing what we know we should do as a witness for Christ, people are perishing.

Rather than walking by or turning a blind eye, we each need to do a heart evaluation. How is our compassion gauge? Do you remember what it was like to be that person who desperately needed help? Who was that person who helped you? Who first introduced you to Jesus? Who was there for your during your darkest hour?

Many have forgotten what it was like to be that one who needed to be reached with the gospel of Jesus Christ, and they have become numb. They are thankful for the blessings they freely enjoy, but forego the opportunity to be a blessing in someone else's life.

How important is it to you to please the one who commissioned you to be a minister of the gospel?

Ephesians 4:1 NKJV, says that God chose you before the foundations of the world. You've been redeemed through His blood and you received forgiveness of sins. That's something to be grateful for.

The great commission is simply sharing the love of God with others. When given the opportunity, are you willing to step out of your comfort zone and share about the goodness of God and bring hope to the hopeless? The only time when God's grace is in vain in a person's life is when their emotions and circumstances become more dominant than the authority of God's word.

God has empowered you to be a witness for Christ. This is not just to save your life but also so you can be a vessel of honor for Him to work through. Your compassion will make a difference for someone, perhaps even a nation. God will always lift up a person who has a willing and obedient heart to serve him. It is the grace of God that qualifies a person to be a witness to others, not a person's abilities or talents.

"Write the vision, make it plain on tablets, that he may run who reads it" (Habakkuk 2:2 NKJV).

My prayer for you is that you may run with a passion and focus in the direction that God has for your life. We need to share with others that there is hope. Share that Jesus is the one who puts the broken pieces of their lives together. He is Christ, the healer who heals, the one who restores our deep emotional wounds. He is the one who gives people a fresh start in life!

No matter what mess you're caught up in today, I want to let you know that God has not given up on you. Just like he did not give up on any of those children in Thailand, He has a perfect plan and purpose that He desires to carry out through your life. The children's future at that orphanage awakened and materialized because someone allowed the compassion of Jesus to be dispensed through their obedience.

Today, some of those children who were rescued from child trafficking are serving the Lord. They're going into remote villages themselves and they're preaching the gospel of the Kingdom. They're testifying about Jesus who picked up the broken pieces of their lives and made them whole once again. They're plucking others out of the fires of hell because they know what it is like to be on the other side, because they were once there.

We ministered alongside some of these young people. And let me tell you, they have a passion for God. They understand their God-given destiny. They have discovered that they are the Moses' to their generation! Meanwhile, the volunteers and missionaries at that orphanage in Thailand are like Pharaoh's daughter. They see the children, and their hearts are so filled with the compassion of God that they do whatever it takes to rescue one more child. They started with one child, and today they have over 100 children at their home, training them in the ways of the Lord, teaching them about the bible and empowering them to go and set their nation free.

"Before I formed you in the womb I knew (and) approved of you (as My chosen instrument), and before you were born I separated and set you apart, consecrating you; (and) I appointed you as a prophet to the nations" (Jeremiah 1:5 AMP).

There's no doubt that God has given you a voice. The call of God is upon your life. His great grace is upon you. He has called you to make a difference, and the compassion of Jesus has been deposited in your heart.

This is a simple message, but with this message comes an impartation of the Holy Spirit for God's compassion to dwell upon the inside of you if you will receive it. You are going to come across many situations where you will have a choice: you can either choose to turn a blind eye and turn a deaf ear, or you can choose to step out in faith and be an extension of God's hands and feet. When that choice comes, I urge you to be His mouthpiece! Boldly share about His unconditional love for people.

We have many things to be thankful for but do we even take a moment to think about those who are less fortunate? Are we willing to sacrifice certain things so that we can be a blessing to others? God wants to activate your faith, ignite your passion, and expand your vision.

"Rescue the perishing; don't hesitate to step in and help. If you say, 'Hey that's none of my business,' will that get you off the hook? Someone is watching you closely you know— Someone not impressed with weak excuses" (Proverbs 24:11 MSG).

This is a message about God's unconditional love and compassion. God loves you with a passion and He will never give up on you. He has great things that He wants to accomplish through your life. Ask the Lord to fill your heart with His love and compassion for people.

Prayer:

"Father, I pray that I would see through the eyes of Jesus. May your love and compassion flood my heart so that I can be a vessel that would bring honor and glory to your Name. I believe that there is an awakening within me to make a difference in my generation. By the grace of God, I will reach my family, friends, and those you place across my path. May your love and compassion for the lost and the brokenhearted fuel me in making a difference in people's lives. In Jesus' name I pray, Amen."

When a spark within you is ignited, there is a passion that burns for the purposes of God.

Chapter 5

SPARK

Even so the tongue is a little member, and it can boast of great things. See how much wood or how great a forest a tiny spark can set ablaze!

James 3:5 AMP

It's amazing how a little spark can ignite a fire, which in turn, can burn down an entire forest. In the same manner, all it takes is a spark of God's word to ignite a fire within our hearts. It can propel us to take on great exploits for the glory of God!

When God's word is embedded in your spirit, you will begin to speak it with conviction and back it with action. That is exactly what we see in the life of David when the children of Israel lined up for battle against the Philistines. No one dared face Goliath, except David.

Then he stood and cried out to the armies of Israel, and said to them, "Why have you come out to line up for battle? Am I not a Philistine, and you the servants of Saul? Choose a man for yourselves, and let him come down to me. If he is able to fight with me and kill me, then we will be your servants. But if I prevail against him and kill him, then you shall be our servants and serve us." And the Philistine said, "I defy the armies of Israel this day; give me a man, that we may fight together." When Saul and all Israel heard these words of the

Philistine, they were dismayed and greatly afraid (1 Samuel 17:8-11 NKJV).

Goliath challenged the armies of Israel for a period of forty days, but no one stepped up to the challenge. Around this time, David visited his three older brothers who were a part of King Saul's army. When David heard the challenge from Goliath, a spark was ignited in his heart. He wondered why no one would fight the Philistine.

Then David began to inquire from the soldiers of King Saul and asked, "What shall be done for the man who kills this Philistine?"

Young David had a distinct voice because he didn't speak like everybody else. There was a boldness and confidence in God that was evident in his life. King Saul soon heard about David's inquiries and sent for him.

At this point, no one believed that David would be able to defeat Goliath. King Saul doubted his qualifications; not even David's own brothers believed. But one thing everyone knew was that although David was not enlisted in the Army, he was the only one up for the challenge. He spoke with a burning conviction in his heart, and he came down to the valley of Elah to face the Philistine. Ultimately, he was the one who slung a stone that struck down the giant Goliath.

"Therefore David ran and stood over the Philistine, took his sword and drew it out of its sheath and killed him, and cut off his head with it. And when the Philistines saw that their champion was dead, they fled." Now, the men of Israel and

Judah arose and shouted and pursued the Philistines. King Saul, the commander of the army, asked, "Who is this youth" (1 Samuel 17:51 NKJV).

Before this war happened, no one knew who young David was. He arose out of obscurity in a time when the Israelites were in desperate need of a leader. Yet, in a moment, God turned the tables in favor of His people.

If you would just fan that spark into a mighty flame like young David, you can conquer anything. David mobilized a stagnated army that had been paralyzed in fear and intimidation. There was a distinct voice of faith that arose amongst the army, and it gave hope to everyone who heard it. While everyone was speaking worry, fear and defeat, David spoke hope, faith and victory! This army of men was mobilized to answer the call to drive out the Philistines.

If you would just dare to trust God, step out in faith, and do what he's called you to do, you will see the power of God move in and through your life. Your spark of conviction has the potential of igniting others to answer the call upon their lives.

****

I remember praying back in 1999, "Father, use me, my God, to win multitudes to Christ. Use me, my God, to preach to the nations of the world."

That was the first time in my life that I started to speak God's word and promises over my life. I prayed and fasted for several days. Though I had never traveled to other countries, except for the Philippines, where I was born, there was a spark that had been ignited on the inside of me to minister to the nations.

At that time, I worked as a janitor at my church. One late night around 11:30 p.m. after I swept and vacuumed the sanctuary, I stood on stage, mounted that pulpit and visualized preaching to the multitudes. I only had one person attending my bible study small group at that time, but that didn't faze me. I continued to declare the promises of God, speaking it over myself out loud when nobody was looking. Gradually, it started to stir within my heart.

"The Spirit of the Lord is upon Me, because He has anointed me to preach the gospel to the poor; He has sent Me to heal the brokenhearted, to proclaim liberty to the captives and recovery of sight to the blind, to set at liberty those who are oppressed; to proclaim the acceptable year of the Lord" (Luke 4:18-19 NKJV).

One day, I shared with Pastor Art, "I don't know what's going on with me, but I have the feeling that I am supposed to go to the nations. Can I go?"

At the time, the schedules just didn't seem to line up, so I concluded in my mind that my desire to go to the nations must have been something I'd conjured myself, rather than God's plan. Because my pastor did not release me at the time, I buried that spark deep within me and instead vowed to myself that I would start reaching out, here in Hawaii.

For the next couple moths, I witnessed to many different neighborhoods on the island and trained many people in my church to share their faith with others.

Just when I'd all but forgotten about my desire to minister abroad, Pastor Art approached me, asking if I'd like to accompany him on a trip to the Philippines.

With Jesus' touch, the spark that once burned in my heart to go to the nations revived in full force.

"Yes!" I said.

Since then I have visited Colombia, Thailand, Japan, South Korea and the Philippines, and I believe that in the future I will have the opportunity to witness to even more nations. It is a desire that God has placed upon my heart.

The first time I traveled to the Philippines was to attend a conference in 2009 with Pastor Art. There were just three of us.

While there, I approached Pastor Art, "The spark is stirring within me again," I told him. "I feel like I need to 'hit the streets.'"

With Pastor Art's support and encouragement, the three of us went out, excited for the opportunity to share Jesus' love.

When we arrived at a community in Manila, I had an intuition to stop, so we stopped walking. It must have been as good a place as any, because within a couple minutes, we had 223 people surrendering their hearts to Christ.

While there, we met an elderly man who had not been able to walk for several years because his legs and joints were severely swollen. We prayed for him, and he started walking! Suddenly, everyone present at the event wanted prayer. The power of God was moving upon the people to heal, so we stayed and prayed for the people for almost four hours.

In 2010, I took another trip to the Philippines. That time we were able to lead 1,700 souls to Christ in 10 days. During one of the services, a man carried in his bedridden daughter, laid her on the cement floor, and asked for prayer. Immediately, we paused the sermon and gathered around to pray for her. Within minutes, the girl got up and started running up and down the aisle of the church!

The power of God was moving that day! At the same meeting, another lady received her sight as one of the other ministers prayed for her. We truly serve a miracle-working God.

The Lord is always looking for vessels who will dare to believe Him at His word. In the 2011 trip, we were able to lead 2,950 people to Christ in the Philippines in 10 days. The following year, we had 30 people join the mission team and had the privilege of leading over 4,000 people to Christ in 10 days as well. Looking back, it all started in 1999 when I first felt the spark to preach to the nations of the world.

Each and every one of us carries a spark inside, meant to ignite others. Has that spark been ignited on the inside of you to reach your community, your city, your nation?

"Even so the tongue is a little member, and it can boast great things. See how much wood or how great a forest a tiny spark can set ablaze!" (James 3:5 AMP)

Where there is no redemptive revelation of God, the people perish. Where there is no vision, the people perish. We can also say it in this way: Where there are no people to rally behind the cause, the vision perishes.

Winning the multitudes takes a vision that can only come from God. We have to visualize its fulfillment in the spirit. Having vision is one of the greatest gifts you can receive from the Lord. When you have vision, you will live your life with a purpose that is so much greater than yourself.

God has a specific plan for each and every one of us that brings honor to His name and positions us to fulfill our God given potential. We all have a significant role to play in seeing the vision to reach the world for Christ fulfilled. It's going to take the church, committed disciples of Christ who have a sense of urgency, to make a difference in this world.

Let's take a look at the life of Nehemiah:
"One of my brethren came with men from Judah; and I asked them concerning the Jews who had escaped, who had survived the captivity and concerning Jerusalem. And they said to me, "The survivors who are left from the captivity in the province are there in great distress and reproach. The wall of

Jerusalem is also broken down, and its gates are burned with fire." So it was, when I heard these words that I sat down and wept, and mourned for many days; I was fasting and praying before the God of heaven" (Nehemiah 1:2-4 NKJV).

Enemies had just attacked Nehemiah's people, and the gates and walls of Jerusalem had been burned and broken down. Imagine losing your home and everything you value— all destroyed along with your entire neighborhood. The people were forced to sleep out in the open without any shelter for their children. They were discouraged, depressed and hopeless regarding their situation.

When Nehemiah heard the news, something broke on the inside of him, and a spark was ignited within him to do something about it. He began to fast and pray for his people for many days. Although he lived comfortably in the King's palace serving as a cupbearer, he could not forget about those who were brokenhearted. He didn't know what to do, but He knew Who to turn to; he turned to God.

When things get difficult in life, many people see God as the last resort for their answers. Meanwhile, Nehemiah put God first. He had a respectable career, but seeing his people in distress was tearing him up on the inside. (That is the spark that I'm writing about.)

Everyday, his mind was consumed with the welfare of his people. And when he appeared before the king, the king questioned why Nehemiah's countenance was sad.

Nehemiah proceeded to tell the king the whole story of what took place back in Jerusalem. And he requested permission to go to Jerusalem that he may rebuild the walls.

He received the king's blessing, but he had no clue where to begin. All he knew was that something inside him had ignited.

When a spark is ignited, there is a cry from within that is stirred. Sometimes, when you get exposed or hear certain things, it drives you to prayer. This is the spark that moves you to action.

And the officials did not know where I had gone or what I had done. I had not yet told the Jews, the priests, the nobles, the officials, or the others who did the work. Then I said to them, "You see the distress that we are in, how Jerusalem lies waste, and its gates are burned with fire. Come and let us build the wall of Jerusalem, that we may no longer be a reproach." And I told them of the hand of my God which had been good to me, and also of the king's words that he had spoken to me. So they said, "Let us rise up and build." Then they set their hands to do this good work (Nehemiah 2:16-18 NKJV).

Vision in the midst of despair brings hope to the people. Nehemiah rallied the leaders and the elders and shared with them a compelling vision that set ablaze the hearts of his people.

Within 52 days, the people were able to rise up and rebuild the walls and gates of Jerusalem. The bible says Eliashib, the high priest, arose. And next to him, the family of Zaccur arose. Next to him, the family of Hassenaah arose. And next to him the family of Meremoth arose. Countless men and women of God began to arise behind this cause that God had instilled within Nehemiah. Although they were faced with many adversities, the spark that was on the inside of them was greater than any outward force that was trying to extinguish it!

I know that there is a spark in you. The adversity and the storms of life are trying to come against you. Sometimes the devil will attempt to sow seeds of doubt and unbelief regarding the promises of God; as negative words are spoken against you. He will get you to second-guess yourself. Know that the spark is too great to be snuffed out by any lies of the enemy.

You have a spark within that you need to guard, protect and nurture. Feed it with the promises of God's word by constantly speaking His promises. When you meditate on God's promises, you get to the place where you become so persuaded that you develop a conviction for the integrity of His word

Just as Saul tried to discourage David from fighting Goliath, people may try to discourage you from fulfilling your plan. They may say you don't have the qualifications or try to convince you that you are insufficient in some way.

Just remember: You may seem insufficient in the eyes of man, but you are more than enough in the eyes of God. As long as you have faith in God and believe, that is all the qualifications you need to overcome any situation!

Against all odds, David carried a burning conviction in his heart regarding God's faithfulness to deliver, that not even the king could persuade him otherwise. His faith in God was undeniable and it gave hope and encouragement to an entire army!

The bible says, David ran towards Goliath. He didn't walk towards the enemy reluctantly. He ran with a burning zeal towards Goliath. As David slung that stone, scripture tells us that the stone sank in Goliath's forehead, and the giant dropped to the ground and fell on his face.

In the midst of victory, David declared Goliath's end before he struck him down saying, "You come to me with a sword, with a spear, and a javelin. But I come to you in the name of the Lord of hosts, the God of the armies of Israel, who you have defied. This day the Lord will deliver you into my hand, and I will strike you and take your head from you. And this day I will give the carcasses of the camp of the Philistines to the birds of the air and the wild beasts of the earth, that the earth may know that there is a God in Israel. Then all this assembly shall know that the Lord does not save with sword and spear; for the battle is the Lord's, and He will give you into our hands" (1 Samuel 17:45-47 NKJV).

David made that declaration of faith before he engaged the enemy. That kind of conviction in the heart is developed through a personal relationship and faith in God. You've got to make your declaration of faith. I want you to visualize yourself like young David or like Nehemiah, who emerged as amazing vessels for the Lord. When the time is right, there will be a stirring, a reviving, a fanning into flame of the spark that is in your heart.

Prayer:

"Father, I have heard your word today. I receive it not as a word from man but as it is in truth, the Word of God. I believe in the holy name of Jesus, I declare that the spark inside of me has been ignited! Holy Spirit, I receive the fresh breath of heaven upon my life now. Fan that spark into a mighty flame that burns away every excuse that has been holding me back from what you have called me to be. I believe that You will be glorified through my obedience. Many people's lives will be touched by your unconditional love for them. I declare breakthrough in my personal walk with God today! I am breaking through in every area of my life in Jesus' name! I arise with the voice of triumph today. I thank you my God for your presence that is reviving my passion to live for you. Today, I cross over into a new dimension of faith. I am conquering new territories. The enemy is fleeing. He has to let go. He's got to release what rightfully belongs to me. I overcome every adversity by the blood of the Lamb, in the name of Jesus. The spark within me is centered upon my intimate relationship with you. I desire more of you in my life, God. In Jesus' Name I pray. Amen."

What you feed yourself is what you will hunger for. Keep yourself filled with God's word.

Chapter 6

HUNGER

"As the deer pants and longs for the water brooks, so I pant and long for you, O God. My inner self thirsts for God, for the living God. When shall I come and behold the face of God?"

Psalms 42:1-2 AMP

We are a three-part being, our physical body, our soul, and our spirit. Our spirit, our inner self, needs nourishment, just like our physical body needs nourishment. What you feed yourself is what you will hunger for. Keep yourself filled with God's word, and you will be fueled for God's call upon your life.

In this chapter, I want to share a couple of examples in the bible of mighty servants of God who had a hunger and thirst for God's presence. The one thing I recognize that every great man and woman of God have in common, is their strong relationship with the Lord.

Let's begin with Moses. God called him to come up to Mount Sinai in order to receive the law and commandments on tablets of stone. He went up to the mountain for 40 days and 40 nights, and he brought along his assistant named Joshua.

While Moses and Joshua were away, the children of Israel sinned against God. The Israelites went against His instructions and created a golden calf—a false idol. When Moses returned from the top of the mountain, he rebuked them and then went to pray on their behalf.

And it came to pass that everyone who sought the Lord went out to the tabernacle of meeting, which was outside the camp. So it was, whenever Moses went out to the tabernacle, that all the people rose, and each man stood at his tent door and watched Moses until he had gone into the tabernacle. And it came to pass, when Moses entered the tabernacle, that the pillar of cloud descended and stood at the door of the tabernacle, and the Lord talked with Moses (Exodus 33:7-9 NKJV).

Moses' devotion and hunger for God set him apart from everybody else in his generation. He had a hunger and thirst for God all the time, whether circumstances were bad or good. He was a man who was in constant fellowship with the Lord, and his example made a tremendous impact in the life of Joshua, who had no idea that he was being prepared to be the next generation leader who was going to carry on the mantle of Moses.

According to Exodus 33:15, Moses desired the presence of God more than the blessing of the Promised Land. For him, there was nothing in this world that could compare with his close relationship with the Lord.

Do you want to know more about God? Is your heart yearning for more of His presence in your life? Everyone has an opportunity to grow as a follower of Christ, but not everyone is willing to pay the price.

A person with a hunger for God will press through every obstacle in their way. They'll press through every accusation. They will not give up on God's promises regardless of how circumstances may appear or how they may feel.

They'll press through every offense, every challenge, every rejection, every trial, every tribulation, every suffering. Why? Because they value the presence of the Lord in their lives more than anything else.

Don't ever forget the spiritual disciplines that brought you to where you are today. If you do not have a daily discipline of growing yourself spiritually, start by reading the bible 10 minutes each day. Create a daily time of reflection where you can ponder on God's word, and apply it to your life. All you need to do is ask God for wisdom and insight to help you to understand His holy scriptures.

****

When I first became a Christian, I dove eagerly into the word of God, often spending hours reading and reflecting on His word. While my friends in the military spent their weekends partying, I remember staying in my tent to read the bible. At that point in my life, I had never read a book from front to back. However, within a couple months, I had devoured the book, reading it cover to cover, including the footnotes.

I realized the Bible was no ordinary book. The word of God inspired and moved me, helping me to examine my life and evaluate the changes I needed to make. God started to do a miraculous work in my heart as He showed me the power of forgiveness.

As I spent time worshipping, singing and praying before the Lord, I would become overwhelmed by His goodness. I really had no idea where to begin or how to develop a spiritual life, but the Holy Spirit started to show me little steps I could take. Sometimes I would find myself in tears, not out of sadness but out of gratitude for His mercy on my life.

Within the next couple of years, I purchased different translations of the bible in order to deepen my understanding. Then I started to learn about the discipline of prayer and fasting. I started a small group bible study, and I fasted each time I prepared myself to minister to people in my bible study group. I wanted to see the people delivered, healed and set free, and I understood that it could only be accomplished in a supernatural way with the presence of the Lord and the power of His word.

Spiritual Hunger is a sign of spiritual health. It doesn't come without taking a good long look at your values and priorities. If something is no longer beneficial for you, you may have to place it at the altar and give them up.

When you commit to set yourself apart for the Lord, He will replace those things that are holding you back from growing with other things that are beneficial. For example, if television, video games or hobbies are holding you back, you may have to give them up in order to experience a heightened desire to hear the voice of His word in your heart.

The apostle Paul had an intense passion for the Lord and forsook everything in order to grow closer in his relationship with God. He embraced God's call to become a minister of the gospel and completely invested himself in sharing His word. In doing so, not only was he able to maintain his spiritual hunger, but he developed it on a daily basis.

"Guard your heart above all else, for it determines the course of your life." (Proverbs 4:23 in the NLT)

Understand that there may be resistance to your hunger. If certain things have tainted your heart, simply humble yourself before the Lord and repent. It's okay to repent; repentance opens the doors to the blessings of the Lord, so that the manifest presence of God can be in your life.

With faith, you can bounce back against every challenge life throws against you. Locate His promises in the scriptures, and as the opportunity presents itself, walk it out in obedience.

I usually speak God's word over my life, then ask the Lord to give me courage to apply it. If the bible tells us that we are to forgive just as He forgave us, then that settles it. Choose to forgive those who have hurt you, regardless of how you feel. In doing so, you prevent the enemy from stealing your spiritual hunger.

God has called us to live by faith and not be governed by our emotions. "Without faith, it is impossible to please God" (Hebrews 11:6 NKJV). Know that each time you apply the word of God and believe His promises, it pleases Him. Your faith and confidence in God will begin to grow, and you will develop a conviction about the truth of God's word.

Commit to speak the language of faith over yourself at all times. Anyone can rehearse the problem and the challenge, but it takes a person of faith to believe God's word and act upon it. When you are feeling sick, declare that you are healed by the stripes of Jesus! (Isaiah 53:5 NKJV) When you are facing financial challenges, speak increase and not lack. (Philippians 4:19 NKJV) We serve a miracle-working God in whom nothing is impossible.

One of the most important things you can do in your personal walk with the Lord is to guard against anything that can contaminate your faith. If you have any offense or bitterness towards someone, take a moment to get right with God and pray.

Here's a simple prayer you can use:
Father, I ask you to forgive me for allowing offense and hurt to linger in my heart. You said that we are to forgive those who persecute us. I choose to forgive those who have hurt me. I pray that you would bless them and reveal yourself to them. I pray that they would come to a right relationship with you. In Jesus' name I pray.

Never leave home without your strong confession of faith. Develop an insatiable desire for the Lord's presence and His word. The word insatiable means it cannot be satisfied. It wants more and more; that's why, even after the Lord spoke to Moses face-to-face, he wanted more of God in his life. He had a passionate pursuit and hunger for more.

Anytime you encounter challenges and handle them correctly, you develop spiritual maturity. When you go through challenging times and you endure, you become stronger, and the hunger for God becomes greater on the inside of you.

Jesus Himself faced challenges, adversities and temptations. He demonstrated by example how to overcome the enemy and walk in victory. Then the devil, taking Him up on a high mountain, showed Him all the kingdoms of the world in a moment of time. And the devil said to Him, "All this authority I will give You, and their glory; for this has been delivered to me, and I give it to whomever I wish. Therefore, if You will worship before me, all will be Yours." And Jesus answered and said to him, "Get behind Me, Satan! For it is written, You shall worship the Lord your God, and Him only you shall serve" (Luke 4:5-8 NKJV).

What did Jesus do? He spoke the Word of God in order to come against the strategies of the enemies. The next time the enemy tries to take dominion over your mind, you've got to speak the Word of the Lord knowing that you have authority and power in Christ Jesus. Seek knowledge and understanding of the word. It is a weapon that God has given us to withstand the enemy called the devil.

Everyone is facing a battle, test or trial. While many are caught up in compromise and complacency, God is raising up a generation of people out of obscurity into purpose-filled lives where signs, wonders and miracles flow readily.

So, how is your hunger and thirst for God? What have you given your appetite over to? Is God still your burning passion?

Hunger is the key to whether or not you are going to pursue God, your call, and your destiny, despite the obstacles that may come your way. It may not be easy, but the return it yields in our lives is well worth it.

Prayer:

"Father, I thank you that I have a hunger within me to know you more intimately than ever before. I choose to guard and protect it from anything that would contaminate my passionate pursuit of You. I believe that through my communion with You; my faith will continue to grow, I will have greater clarity of purpose, and I will flourish in the call that You have placed upon my life. It's all centered upon my personal relationship with You Lord. In Jesus' name. Amen."

Have an urgency for reaching those who are dear to your heart. Missed opportunities don't always come back around.

Chapter 7

URGENCY

Herald and preach the Word! Keep your sense of urgency (stand by, be at hand and ready), whether the opportunity seems to be favorable or unfavorable. Whether it is convenient or inconvenient, whether it is welcome or unwelcome...

2 Timothy 4:2 AMP

It was a Sunday morning, and I was scheduled to take the first flight to Kahului Maui, which meant that I had to be at the airport by 4 a.m. I only lived 10 minutes from the airport, so I assumed it wouldn't be a problem. Unfortunately, when I woke up, I had exactly 55 minutes before the plane was scheduled to depart. I had slept through the alarm.

To make matters worse, I'd also forgotten to check in online the night before my flight, and when I tried to do so in the morning, the website indicated it was too late; I had to see the attendant at the airport. With that, I quickly woke my wife to drop me off, got dressed, brushed my teeth, grabbed my backpack, and we ran out the door.

On our way to the airport, it seemed like every traffic light took twice as long as usual to turn green. My concern got so bad that I was tempted to run a couple of red lights. (I didn't.)

As soon as we arrived at the airport, I gave my wife a kiss and then sprinted towards the ticketing counter. The attendant was able to issue me my ticket, but I still had to get through customs and security. Thank God the line that day wasn't long! By the grace of God, I was able to make it to the plane on time.

Have you ever been pressed for time? Maybe you had an interview scheduled for the dream job you had always wanted. You are dressed to impress and ready for any question the interviewer might throw your way. Then you realize you can't find the keys to your car, and you are already stretched for time. You find yourself scrambling throughout your house in an attempt locate your misplaced keys. Finally, you call for a taxi only to be placed on hold.

That is not a situation any of us would like to be in! The point that I want to make is that too many people wait until the last minute to share Christ with a family member. They are well versed on what to say but don't take the time to share it until it's too late.

One thing is for sure, we will not live forever on Earth. The time will come when our life will expire, and we will enter into eternity. The question is, where will you spend it? Where will your family, friends and relatives be?

Just as people are destined to die once, and after that to face judgment, so Christ was sacrificed once to take away the sins of many; and He will appear a second time, not to bear sin, but to bring salvation to those who are waiting for Him. (Hebrews 9:27 NIV)

None of us knows when our last day will be, and as a result, many cross over to eternity without having an opportunity to receive Jesus as their Savior. I don't wish it upon anyone to experience that uncertainty on their deathbed, not knowing what to do or whom to reach out to in order to make things right with God. You must embrace a sense of urgency for reaching everyone you hold dear to your heart, because missed opportunities don't always come back around.

****

One day I asked myself, "If I only had thirty minutes left in my life, how would I live it out?" I started to ponder the "sense of urgency" the Apostle Paul instructed Timothy to keep in his a witness for Christ. I went over to a nearby community park, closed my eyes and said, "Holy Spirit, I want every witnessing effort to count, so I ask you to lead me and guide me."

When I opened my eyes, there were several groups of people that tugged at my heart. However, at that moment, negative thoughts began to bombard my mind, and I felt the devil trying to intimidate me through fear. My heart started racing, and I felt so nervous. I had no assurance that they would be open to what I had to share.

"No, no, no!" I said to myself, "I will not fear, in Jesus' name!" Then I recalled 2 Timothy 1:7 NKJV: For God has not given us a sprit of fear, but of power and of love and of a sound mind.

Without any further hesitation, I stood up and walked towards a couple sitting at a nearby picnic table. Based on the young man's build, my mental math indicated he could knock me out with one punch if he for some reason got offended.

As I approached them I hid my smart phone, made sure my wallet was secure, and tightened my belt in case I needed to bolt for safety.

"Sir, do you know what time it is?" I asked as I drew near. (Though I knew what time it was, I used the opening line as a way to initiate conversation.)

"Yeah, it's 3:15 p.m." he responded.

Emboldened by the man's response, I began asking the couple questions about spiritual things.

"Has anyone ever shared with you just how much God loves you?" I asked. Then I asked for their names.

"Oh, my name is Jessica," said the woman.

"And my name is Bobby," said the man.

"Oh, hi! Nice to meet you," I responded.

As I continued ministering to them, the conviction of the Holy Spirit started to grip the young woman's heart.

Eventually, she stopped me. "My name is not really Jessica," she admitted. "And to be honest with you, I'm high right now," said the man.

"That's not a problem at all," I told them, eager to make sure they didn't feel like they were being judged.

In my experience, many people immediately disconnect when they feel they're being looked down upon. Instead of judging them, I began to share my message about the goodness of God and about who Jesus is.

As I ministered to them, I realized the man spoke very limited English. He could understand and say a few words, but English was definitely not his first language. Rather than letting myself become discouraged, I led him to Christ through his girlfriend who translated for him in their own dialect. She was praying in the Micronesian language, and he repeated the prayer after her. That afternoon, they both sincerely surrendered their hearts to Jesus.

Afterwards, I approached and ministered to eight more people in a period of thirty minutes. I really took the time to heard their concerns and challenges in life. As I shared about the promises of God's word, their hearts were encouraged and touched in a mighty and powerful way.

All God really expects from us is our obedience to share Christ with others. We trust and leave the results to God. He is the one who convicts people of sin and turns their hearts to Jesus.

"And when He has come, He will convict the world of sin, and of righteousness and of judgment." (John 16:8 NKJV).

The responsibility of convicting is the Holy Spirit's alone; we are simply His messengers. All He needs from us is to be is an extension of His hands and His feet, and to be the mouthpiece for Jesus. God is simply looking for people who will avail themselves to reach out to someone.

When you have a sense of urgency to minister God's love and salvation, you will minister to people wherever you are. I have led people to Christ at a park, in the elevator, in the men's restroom, at the bus stop, and even at a restaurant.

One time my friend Jarmal and I were playing basketball at the park, and we noticed one of the players was limping after the game.

"You know what, God wants to heal your leg," said Jarmal. "What's wrong with your leg?"

The man replied, "Oh, man, I injured it a while back."

"Would you like for me to pray for you?" asked Jarmal.

The man consented, so we prayed for him. When we were done, we told him, "Jump on your hurt foot. God's healing power is upon you right now."

"Wow, the pain is gone!" said the man. This healing experience opened up an opportunity for us to minister to everybody else on the court.

"And they went out and preached everywhere, the Lord working with them and confirming the word through the accompanying signs" (Mark 16:20 NKJV).

We can bring the manifestation of the power of God by daring to step out in faith according to His promises. The Lord is our partner and confirms what He has spoken in His word when we simply share the truth with others.

In the later days of the Apostle Paul, he was charging his disciple, Timothy, and he said, 2 Timothy 4:1-2 AMP "I charge (you) in the presence of God and of Christ Jesus, Who is to judge the living and the dead and by (in light of) His coming and His kingdom: Herald and preach the Word! Keep your sense of urgency (stand by, be at hand and ready), whether the opportunity seems to be favorable or unfavorable. Whether it is convenient or inconvenient, whether it is welcome or unwelcome..."

Know that there will be times when people will not welcome you sharing your faith. But that should not deter you from taking an opportunity to do so. Know that it is not you that they are rejecting but the one who sent and commissioned you, Jesus Christ Himself. So learn to not take it personally when you are given an unfavorable response. Continue to love on everyone and be that good example.

One thing that is lacking in some churches today is an urgency to spread the gospel of Jesus Christ. Some believers slowly sink into this state of tepidness and never get around to sharing about the love of God with those who desperately need Him.

In today's fast-paced, distraction-filled world, how do we keep this sense of urgency—especially when it's something that might be easily lost? Sometimes we just get caught up in the busyness of life and find no time to serve the Lord.

We prioritize our life according to what we value, which begs the question: Is there more to life than just being happy? I think there is. It's to live a life of purpose! Let God's purposes be at the center of it all. When all is said and done, the only thing that matters is what we did with what God called us to do as a disciple of Christ.

Back in 2009, I met a world-renowned evangelist and asked him a question, "When you speak at different churches, what kind of spiritual discipline do you demand of yourself? How many days of prayer and fasting do you do?" I wanted to learn as much as I possibly could from this man of God.

His response? "It's a lifestyle!"

So now when people ask me, "What does your spiritual discipline look like? How long do you pray? How often do you fast?" I just answer, "It's a lifestyle!" I adopted this particular mindset because it is so true. This is a part of our makeup in Christ and who we are.

So how do you keep your sense of urgency? You make reaching others with the gospel of Jesus your lifestyle. Embrace it as a daily discipline not out of obligation, but out of a genuine desire to please God and to be a blessing to others. Whether or not the opportunity is favorable, step out and do it. We must seize every opportunity the Lord gives us.

"For what is your life? It is even a vapor that appears for a little time and then vanishes away." (James 4:14 NKJV).

Our life is but a vapor in comparison to eternity. Sometimes we cannot take back those missed opportunities that we allow to pass us by. Whether we are a new believer, a seasoned believer or a pastor at a local church, we all should be a witness for the Lord Jesus Christ.

****

I used to live in downtown Honolulu, and I would sometimes walk my dogs during my break before I needed to be at my next meeting that evening. I recall a time when I was pressed for time; but even in these moments, God has an assignment for us.

As I passed by the bus stop, I sensed a tugging of the Holy Spirit upon my heart to minister to a group of men. I tried to reason with myself about not being late for my meeting, but I couldn't shake off what was stirring in my spirit. So, I approached that bus stop and began witnessing to everyone there. To make a long story short, right when I was about to lead them in the prayer of salvation, the bus arrived.

When the bus driver opened the doors, I turned to the people and asked, "Do you want to receive Jesus in your life or get on that bus?"

Because the Holy Spirit had so touched their hearts, they decided to catch the next bus. Together, we prayed the sinner's prayer, and the people received Jesus into their hearts. God wants to perform miracles in people's lives, He's just waiting for the moment when someone will share Christ with them.

There are many people who are looking for answers, looking for hope and encouragement. Sometimes those opportunities come at the most inconvenient time. What I have discovered is that the more you yield yourself to the prompting of the Holy Spirit, the more you will be able to identify those opportunities and keep that sense of urgency burning in your heart.

When was the last time you did something out of the ordinary in order to reach people with Jesus' message? If you have lost that desire to reach out to others, know that God wants to pour out a fresh anointing, a fresh touch of His presence upon your life. He wants your heart to be flooded with His love and compassion for the hurting, the broken and those who have lost hope. Let the gift of God be stirred up inside of you.

"Therefore I remind you to stir up the gift of God which is in you through the laying on of my hands" (2 Timothy 1:6 NKJV).

One day, a friend of mine who is a very passionate witness for Christ witnessed to two Japanese tourist girls in Waikiki. He approached them and asked, "Do you know about Jesus?"

"Oh no, we don't believe in God," they replied.

My friend didn't give up easily; but at the end of it all, they still didn't believe.

"Thank you for your time," he told them. "Do you mind if I pray for you?"

They agreed, and as he prayed for them, the two girls experienced the goodness of God's presence; they began to tear up. Sometimes when God touches a person's soul, they are so overwhelmed that they become emotional. Truly, when you're confident about whom you serve, God will confirm His word.

Another time I sat down to eat at a restaurant with some friends. While we were submitting our orders, one of our church members was going table-to-table saying, "Hi, what's your name?"

Some customers replied, "Oh, we're eating."

"That's fine," she said. "Keep on eating. I just want to minister to you."

In her persistence, she was able to lead them to the Lord. That evening, they received Jesus Christ as their personal Lord and Savior.

One of the couples that joined us for lunch was really blessed because the couple that had just surrendered their lives to Jesus was a neighbor of theirs. She had known them for many years, but, out of fear of rejection, she had never taken the time to share Jesus with them.

Your conviction is measured by your corresponding action. It enables you to overcome the spirit of fear and intimidation. Many people regress into a state of lukewarmness when it comes to witnessing and sharing Christ with others. Make a decision to be unashamed of the gospel, and God will grant you the courage.

You don't have to be eloquent in how you share about Jesus, you just have to be willing and genuine. Each time you step out in faith to witness to others, you fan the flame of urgency within you to make a difference. Be God's answer for humanity's cry. Don't be a bystander any longer, but possess an urgency as a witness. There are so many people waiting on the other side of your obedience. Step out of your comfort zone and be the person who God has called you to be. Never lose that sense of urgency.

Prayer:
"Father, I no longer want to be a bystander. I want to be a bold witness for Jesus. I want to be empowered with the Holy Spirit to share the love of Jesus with my family, friends and relatives. I want to have an urgency burning in my heart. I awaken my faith from a state of lukewarmness. I'm going do my part! I'm not going to allow an opportunity to share Christ with my loved ones pass me by any longer. Thank you Lord that you have given me courage and a sense of urgency. In Jesus' name I pray. Amen."

Allow God to enlarge your heart for souls, and you will find yourself making a difference in the lives of others.

Chapter 8

ENLARGE MY HEART

When He looked out over the crowds, His heart broke. So confused and aimless they were, like sheep with no shepherd.
Matthew 9:36 MSG

I remember I was at our leaders' meeting with Pastor Art several weeks before Easter, and he was sharing about enlarging our hearts to reach out to the lost. This reminded me of a story in the book of Luke chapter 24. Jesus walked on the road to Emmaus with His two disciples, and they did not recognize Him until He revealed Himself. When He left their company, the disciples said, "Did not our heart burn within us while He talked with us on the road, and while He opened the Scriptures to us?" There was a stirring within their hearts as Jesus ministered to them the scriptures. I can relate to those early disciples because what my pastor shared that night stirred and enlarged my heart to reach out.

My heart burned with a desire to share Christ with others that very evening, and as soon as the meeting concluded, I prayed to God, "Lord, on my way home tonight, I pray that you would give me the opportunity to lead at least 20 people to Christ."

It was already 9:30 p.m., and my wife was already waiting for me to get home, so there was a sense of urgency within me. I started searching for a big group of people while driving through my neighborhood. Since I was quickly approaching my home, I was resigned that the opportunity would not take place that night. Then I turned the last corner and saw about fifteen people walking out from the basketball court!

"Yes, this is the opportunity I asked the Lord for!" I said to myself as I pulled to the side of the road and parked my car.

"Lord, give me the very words to speak as I endeavor to reach out to them," I prayed. Then I stepped out of my car and introduced myself.

"Hey guys, how's it going?" I said. I tried to learn their names as best as I could, and then I got straight to the point. If I didn't connect with them right away, I knew the opportunity would be lost.

"Has anybody shared with you how much you mean to God and that He loves you very much?" I asked.

Disinterest was plastered to their faces, and their body language screamed, "We don't want to hear this stuff." To make matters more challenging, no one really responded to my questions.

However, with God in my corner, I wasn't about to give up that easily. I knew He wanted to touch their hearts and had given me this opportunity to reach these people, so I tried a different approach: I started speaking to them in Tagalog since they were all Filipinos.

As I spoke to them in our native tongue, their responses became more favorable, "Oh, Pilipino ka pala. Kamusta na pare?" (Translation: "Oh, you're Filipino? How are you doing my friend?")

After switching languages, I was able to connect with them immediately and minister to them about God's unconditional love. They became very open and receptive. I shared with them about the good news of salvation and all 15 of them accepted Jesus Christ into their hearts willingly.

One of them had a car, and the rest of them were going to walk home. So I said, "You know what, I've got a full-size SUV. You can all hop in, and I can drive you home." Somehow, they were all able to fit in my SUV. I dropped them home at their neighborhood and decided to hang out for a bit.

We were all invited into the house, and I seized the opportunity to minister to the parents as well. We had a great time of fellowship. When I drove back home, I also led the security guards at our building to Christ. In the end, 20 people experienced God's love and mercy that night.

There are many people who will be blessed by your obedience to share the love of God with them. Don't give up so easily. All you need to do is allow God to enlarge your heart, and take that step of faith. He will give you wisdom and the very words to speak.

****

"Today, salvation has come to this house, because he also is a son of Abraham (speaking of Zacchaeus). For the Son of Man has come to seek and to save that which was lost" (Luke 19:9-10 NKJV).

Jesus entered Jericho, and there was a man named Zacchaeus, who was the chief tax collector. He was very wealthy but had gained his wealth by collecting more than what was required and cheating other people. However, there was a time in his life when he sought to see who Jesus was. One time, when Jesus was in town, Zacchaeus climbed up a sycamore tree so he could better spot Jesus.

When Jesus came to the spot where Zacchaeus was waiting, Jesus looked up at him and said, "Zacchaeus, come down immediately for today I must stay at your house."

Since Jesus was everything that represented righteousness, many townspeople complained that Jesus had gone to be the guest of a sinner, but Jesus was comfortable going against the accepted norm in His culture.

In the presence of Jesus, Zacchaeus had a change of heart and repented of his evil ways. He promised to give half of his goods to the poor and to restore anything he'd taken by false accusation fourfold. And that is why Jesus declared, "Today, salvation has come to this house" (Luke 19:8-9 NKJV).

Jesus set out in ministry to personally pursue those who didn't have it all together. He freely helped those who had made mistakes in their lives and those who had hurt many people. But God gives everyone the opportunity to have a fresh start in life through repentance. Through faith in Jesus, anyone can receive forgiveness and live a life free from guilt and condemnation.

Our charge is to enlarge our heart for people no matter what their shortcomings may be. There are multitudes in a state of brokenness that are void of hope. When we allow the compassion of Jesus to be real in our life, we become an extension of His hands and feet. Through our obedience of sharing our faith with others, they, too, can receive salvation and forgiveness of sin.

Zacchaeus was the worst tax collector, and at one point the Apostle Paul considered himself the worst sinner. Can you identify with either Zacchaeus or the Apostle Paul? Maybe you used to be someone with a foul mouth, a violent temperament, bitterness or hatred, but God had mercy on your life. This is what the Apostle Paul was expressing when he said, "I thank Christ Jesus my Lord, Who had mercy on me."

If it was a priority for Jesus to seek and to save the lost, shouldn't it be a priority for each and every one of us who profess to be a follower of Christ?

Absolutely. You don't have to memorize every scripture in the bible to be qualified to reach others. All you need is willingness, and God will enlarge your heart and fill it with His love and compassion for people.

****

On my first mission trip to Japan in 2010, I was fully aware that there would be opposition to what we were about to do. Every Japanese believer I spoke with from our church gave me the impression it would be very difficult because of the mindset of the Japanese culture.

I believe that the love of Jesus is the most powerful force in the world and that it can break through any cultural barrier. Rather than allow myself to get discouraged, I said to myself, "I am going to put this to the test by the power of the Holy Spirit!" I vowed to seize whatever opportunity I encountered to share Christ. I did not speak Japanese, but I made an effort to learn some phrases so I could connect with them.

On the flight to Tokyo, I sat beside a couple and began to practice the new Japanese phrases I had learned. Amazingly, they actually lived in Yokohama, which is where our church plant is located.

After a couple minutes of conversation, the woman started weeping because of the goodness of God. I simply showed them some videos of our outreaches in Japan and used it as an open door to share Christ.

When you allow God to enlarge your heart for souls, you will step out and do what God needs you to do. Following my example, some of the Japanese volunteers who had joined us on the trip resolved to start ministering to the people sitting next to them as well. Your example can serve as an inspiration for others to step out in faith.

When you enlarge your heart for humanity, the Holy Spirit will lead you, and sometimes you will need to go against cultural norms. Everywhere we went in Japan, we had to be with somebody who was familiar with the public transit. (There are so many train routes in Japan that we could have easily gotten lost.) Each time we got on the train, we noticed passengers kept to themselves. They were either reading, sleeping, or on their smartphones. I did not see any interaction amongst them at all. Just imagine a train full of people with hardly any room to move around and nobody is talking. All you hear is the train intercom letting you know what the next stop is.

I approached people and decided to initiate a conversation.

"How are you doing? What's your name?" I asked in English.

The translator I was with informed me that they didn't speak English, so I had her translate to them a question: "Is it true that people have jumped in front of trains to commit suicide here in Japan?"

The people looked at me and said, "You know, we don't talk about that stuff, but yes it's true."

Then I said, "What do you think happens to them after?" This opened up a conversation about spiritual and eternal matters. Then I shared that all throughout the world, people are looking for hope, and it is found only in Jesus.

On another train ride to our destination, I decided to practice my Japanese with the girl who sat next to me.

"Hi, what's your name?" I asked her in my best Japanese.

"Honomi," she said.

"Hi, Honomi," I said. "My name is Wally. Do you speak English?"

"Very little," she replied.

"Oh, I'm also learning Japanese. The same way you're trying to learn English, I am learning Japanese," I told her (this time in English). Then I fascinated her with the few Japanese words and phrases I'd learned, including 'Ohayo Gozaimas' (which means good morning), 'Konnichiwa' (good afternoon), 'konbanwa' (good evening), 'sumimasen' (excuse me, sorry), 'arigato gozaimas' (thank you very much)."

"Wow!" she exclaimed, clearly impressed.

"May I ask you a question?" I ventured, using one of the first sentences I'd ever learned in Japanese.

She could understand but she could not really converse back to me. So I continued, "Imamadeni iesusamaga anata-no-kotowo dore dake aishi-teiruka kiitakoto arismaska?"

"Wow," she said, staring back at me.

Basically, I'd said, "Has anyone shared with you how much Jesus Christ loves you?"

One interesting thing about the Japanese language is that there isn't a word for 'Love.' I asked my friend and translator, how do they tell somebody, 'I love you'?" And she said, "They don't." They go throughout a lifetime never hearing from their parents 'I love you.' To the Japanese, words are cheap, while actions speak volumes. In their eyes, anyone can say whatever they wish but genuine affection is communicated through actions.

And so the girl who I was witnessing to in Japanese asked me, "How can I know that Jesus loves me?" I substituted a slang word for love in Japanese since they didn't have a word for it in order to best communicate the gospel.

"The bible tells us that God demonstrated His love for us in that while we were yet sinners, Jesus Christ died for our sins," I replied. This girl was ready to receive Christ, so we prayed for her right there, on that train.

At that point, I took note and said to myself, "You know what, Japan is not impossible." The gospel that we preach in the United States is the same gospel that we preach in Japan. The message of the cross is the power of God unto salvation to those who believe.

There are many people we must reach with the love of Jesus. This could be your mom, dad, brothers, sisters, husband, wife, children, uncles, aunts, cousins, and friends. Enlarging your heart for humanity begins with a willingness to be a vessel for the Lord. Many people are oblivious to the reality of eternal life. They do not realize that someone laid their life down for their salvation, healing, and deliverance. People need to know who that someone is, and His name is Jesus.

****

"Deliver those who are drawn toward death, and hold back those stumbling to the slaughter" (Proverbs 24:11 NKJV).

The message translation says, "Rescue the perishing, don't hesitate to step in and help." Unfortunately, many people don't. They see a person struggling, or a person in need of the love of Jesus, but they are not moved to the point where they step into the mess of those people's lives and share Christ's message of hope. Jesus is the only One who can turn our lives around. We must not be a silent bystander. The world needs to hear who Jesus is.

What is it going to take for local churches to enlarge their hearts for humanity and be the mighty vessels that God has called them to be? I believe that we need to come into contact with the lost. Jesus prayed for people, but He did more than pray. He went about doing good and healing those who were oppressed by the enemy. He went about healing the sick, setting captives free and preaching the good news about the kingdom of God. This is what we must all do.

One night, I took a team that I had been mentoring to the local shopping mall near my house back here in Hawaii. As my team looked on, I approached a group of men standing in front of the liquor store and said, "How's it going guys?"

The men stared at me but didn't say a word.

Finally, someone spoke up and asked, "What do you want?"

I introduced myself and endeavored to find common ground. Then I said, "I want to ask you a question. If a person commits suicide, what do you think happens to him?"

One of the guys replied, "He'll go to hell."

"Well what if someone else asked you, 'how can you get to heaven?', what would you say?" I asked him.

He replied, "Be good and go to church."

"Actually, it's a lot simpler than that," I shared with them. "The bible says that if you believe in your heart and confess with your mouth that Jesus Christ died for your sins and rose again on the third day, you shall be saved."

After that, I taught them about their need of repentance and forgiveness. As we continued our conversation, other people started to gather around us, curious to learn what was going on.

"Oh, oh, what's going on over here?" they wondered.
"I am just sharing with them about Jesus," I said, as the group grew larger.

By the time we were done, eight men accepted Christ into their lives right in front of the liquor store. I invited them to attend my church, so they could continue to grow and flourish in their Christian walk, and they were very grateful.

After I had modeled the example for my team; I challenged them.

"We are going to do some witnessing for the next thirty minutes," I told them. "In that time, I want you guys to go out and share Christ with everybody here in this shopping mall."

After thirty minutes, they had ministered to over fifty people, and many had accepted Jesus.

Another time, my friend and I went to a place that was referred to as a hot spot for gang and drug activities. As we approached a group of gang members drinking in their garage, they started surrounding us as if to say, "Who are these guys rolling up on us? Who do they think they are?" Then, one dude lifted up his shirt to expose the large cut across his abdomen.

"What's up, man?" he said.

My first impression was that he was trying to intimidate me with a stab wound; but then again, it may have been from a recent surgery. Regardless, I took the opportunity to share about Jesus.

The moment I started saying "Jesus," their demeanor changed dramatically. Suddenly, everybody in that group started putting their liquor and marijuana away, saying "Hey, we have a man of God over here." After about ten minutes, they each surrendered their lives to Christ.

The gospel is really a simple message, but it has great power to touch even the hardest of hearts. You don't have to be a theologian in sharing about the message of the Cross. The Holy Spirit will bring conviction upon the hearts of sinners when you share about the love of God for them. All He needs you to do is step out and obey.

The greatest miracle of all is when a person surrenders his or her heart over to Jesus. One moment you are having a conversation with someone who wants to smack your face, then a shift happens and that person is now praying to accept Jesus Christ. That is the power of God!

When you allow God to enlarge your heart, you will not fear. You will be more focused on the well being of people's spiritual condition. Your heart will be filled with compassion to share about the God who helped change your life.

What kind of Christian do you want to be? God has a deep longing for the lost that only you can personally fulfill. This longing is for souls to be saved. The love of Jesus does not exclude anyone, no matter what his or her background may be. We must see through the outward appearance and see each person we come across as someone who God is longing to be in relationship with. We can each reach someone. Pray for those who God has placed upon your heart to reach and expect an opportune time to present itself. God will give you the courage to share your testimony of what the Lord has done for you.

There may be places in your community where you do not feel safe. In those circumstances, it is important for you to pray for the salvation of those who do not have Christ in their lives, and you will be doing your part to bring about change. God is looking for someone who is willing to be a light in the midst of darkness. He will enlarge your heart for souls in your city and beyond.

The man who had been freed from the demons begged to go with Him. But Jesus sent him home, saying, "No, go back to your family, and tell them everything God has done for you." So he went all through the town proclaiming the great things Jesus had done for him" (Luke 8:38-39 NLT).

You may not know what's going in people's lives when you come across them, but God does. He desires to reach them through your obedience. We are God's messengers to this generation. Let's not disconnect ourselves from hurting humanity. This is not the time for us to remain silent. Many have neglected the Great Commission of reaching their world for Christ because they have become more focused on themselves. Allow God to enlarge your heart for souls, and you will find yourself truly making a difference in countless people's lives.

Prayer:
"Father, I thank you for your love and mercy that you have demonstrated towards me. Help me to never forget about your heart for humanity. I pray that I would be sensitive to your guidance each time I come across someone who has been crying out to you. I avail myself to be that vessel that you can

minister through. Enlarge my Heart for people so I do not witness out of a religious obligation, but out of a genuine desire to please you and to touch people's lives. In Jesus' name I pray. Amen."

Only God can light a fire in your heart for souls; but it is your sole responsibility to keep that fire burning.

Chapter 9

KEEP YOUR LAMP BURNING

Be dressed ready for service and keep your lamps burning, like servants waiting for their master to return from a wedding banquet, so that when he comes and knocks they can immediately open the door for him.

Luke 12:35-36 NIV

I remember working in the secular arena back in 1999. Even then, I had a burning passion to win the lost and was fueled by God's love to share Christ with others. Even through I didn't have any formal evangelistic training at the time, I was able to win the entire morning shift, swing shift and the graveyard shift where I worked to Jesus.

Later I went onto another company and worked with a lot of worldly people who liked to use profanity and talk about lustful things. After about two weeks of praying for them, God gave me an opportunity to share about Jesus. I took out my little pocket bible during our lunch break and started reading.

"This is my bible," joked one of the guys, as he showed off a porn magazine he had brought to work.

Since many of them were married, I decided to start with a question.

"Do you ever wonder why wives cheat on their husbands? They connect with someone over the Internet, develop a soul tie, and the next thing you know they want a divorce. Do you ever wonder why some of them find their children caught up in sexual promiscuity? They enter into one relationship after another, only to end up with a broken heart. They feel used and develop a low self-image about themselves. The bible tells us that men are the head of the home. They are to be the protector, provider, and priest of their family. But instead of fulfilling their God-given responsibility, they open the door to unclean spirits in their home. They don't realize that what they are tampering with is affecting their family."

With that, I started to share about the goodness of God and His plan for their lives. After I finished, their hearts were touched and in one accord they all surrendered their hearts to Jesus. Right there in the middle of our job site, during our lunch break, we gathered around a table and prayed the Sinner's Prayer. Though I did not have any formal training, I did not let that hold me back. I was so moved by God's love to see these men saved that I stepped out of my comfort zone and trusted God for the results.

"Therefore settle it in your hearts not to meditate beforehand on what you will answer; for I will give you a mouth and wisdom which all your adversaries will not be able to contradict or resist" (Luke 21:14-15 NKJV).

I believe that God can reach many people through your obedience to share your faith. All it takes is a willing and obedient heart, and God will help you. What he did through me, he will do through you. You are God's ambassador. Let your light shine before men and let them experience the goodness of God when you share about what the Lord has done in your life.

During a workout at the gym, I ran into a man I led to Christ many years ago in 1999 at my security job. This was the very first person I won to the Lord. I remember being so nervous about stepping out in faith to share Christ for the first time. I had to pray a lot just to build up enough courage to speak to him about God's unconditional love.

But here's what happened: When I did, this man wept and accepted Jesus into his heart! When he left to do his security routes, I jumped up and down, celebrating. Yes! What a great feeling it is to lead someone to Christ! I will never forget that experience.

"I say to you that likewise there will be more joy in heaven over one sinner who repents than over ninety nine just person who need no repentance" (Luke 15:7 NKJV).

The main thing we need to remember is our responsibility to be obedient to the great commission. I have led many to Christ at outreaches, missions and church services. But the ones that I remember the most are the one-on-one opportunities I've been given to personally lead individuals to Christ.

Every Christian can experience the joy of knowing that you have made an eternal difference in someone's life. And in doing so, you also touch the heart of our Heavenly Father by fulfilling His desire to see the lost saved.

When we become an example for others to follow, we will be one step closer to revival taking place in our city. When our children carry the heart of the Father, we will revolutionize and change the culture of this world. But it has to be real, first and foremost, in all of our hearts. We should no longer live for ourselves, our own selfish desires, but we should live for the one who died and rose again for our sakes. There's a multitude of people out there who have not yet encountered God's unconditional love.

People need to hear the gospel because they are living with guilt and condemnation due to their past. They have not been able to live the abundant life that God always intended for them to live. They are waiting for men and women of God, such as yourself, to present to them that good news.

After I finished my service in the Marine Corps, I decided to stay in Hawaii. I attended a business college briefly, where I could not help but preach in every single one of my classes. I don't know how I did it, but I shared the gospel in my computer class, my English class and my Business class. Every class I attended, I took the opportunity to share about the goodness of God.

On the day I was assigned to give my final presentation, I requested that we move the presentation from the classroom to the cafeteria. I wanted to go where there were a lot of people.

Although the request was a bit unorthodox, my teacher agreed, and I got to preach the gospel to everyone in the cafeteria through a talk-show format.

Shortly after college, I began leading some young adults at our church. I taught them how to pray and how to share their faith with others. Among other activities, I'd frequently take a group of people to the nearby university to witness on campus.

I modeled the example on how to minister to people. I would choose a group on the college campus and introduce myself, looking for common ground before I began to witness. The team I took with me would observe from a distance, and once I had prayed for the people, I would instruct my team to venture out and do the same. Then we'd fill our church shuttles and bring the college students over to our Friday night services. It was such a joy to see those college students receive Jesus into their lives.

However, there were times when I found that my desire to reach the lost wasn't burning as strongly as it had in the beginning. I knew what I was supposed to do as a follower of Christ, but the drive to do it wasn't as strong as before. Then I came across a passage in Luke 12:35 NKJV during my devotion, and it revived a fire within me: Jesus said, "Be dressed ready for service and keep your lamps burning..."

After reading that passage, I realized that I'd allowed myself to enter into a state of lukewarmness and that the lamp that once burned in me so strongly had been reduced to a distant memory of what once was. To reignite my passion, I asked the

Lord to forgive me and to revive that fire in my heart once again.

If you find yourself in a place where you do not have the desire to see your loved ones saved, ask the Lord to ignite that fire within you. Many times we get caught up in compromise, complacency, or just plain busyness in life.

When that happens, all you need to do is step out of your comfort zone, and take the first step. The Lord will give you boldness and give you the very words to speak in that very moment.

"But when they deliver you up, do not worry about how or what you should speak. For it will be given to you in that hour what you should speak; for it is not you who speak, but the Spirit of your Father who speaks in you" (Matthew 10:19 NKJV).

****

In 2012, I took a team on a mission trip to the Philippines, and we conducted many outreaches. We must have gone through at least 20 different outreach sites and several churches.

The first person I assigned to minister was named Hunter. He is six foot four, and he preached right in the middle of Tondo, the ghetto of the ghettos in the Philippines. It has one of the highest crime rates in the world, with almost one murder each week. This is his account of what happened at that outreach:

"As I sat on the bus, with my palms sweaty and heart racing, I quietly thanked God for His grace and mercy. Just a few minutes ago, I was calm and at ease, why such a sudden difference? Well, my leader Pastor Wally informed me that I would be ministering at the outreach that day. The crazy thing is that we were only 5 minutes away from the location. That's one thing I've learned from being under his leadership— we must be ready in season and out of season. We should always be ready to share the good news about the love and grace of our Savior. The location we were headed to was one of the most dangerous and poverty stricken areas in all the Philippines called Tondo. As we got closer, I thought to myself, I'm 6'4 and white, so in other words I'm going to stick out like a sore thumb! "Well," I said to myself, "If I go out, this is the way to go out, preaching the gospel!" I wanted to call my mom briefly and tell her that I loved her, but it was too late. The bus had just stopped, and we were getting out. I put all my trust in God and the great grace He supplies. I prayed, "None of me and all of you." God came through in a mighty and powerful way. I preached the gospel with boldness and many people gave their hearts to the Lord. That was an experience I will remember for the rest of my life! I will always be thankful to Pastor Wally for giving me an opportunity that forever changed my life and hundreds of others who received Jesus that day."

Was he nervous? You better believe it! But because he yielded himself to the work of the Holy Spirit and kept that lamp burning within his heart, he was able to rise to the occasion and be the vessel that God worked through to bless that community.

Once you open your mouth for Jesus, the boldness of a lion comes forth, and you are transformed into a different person. This is called the anointing of the Holy Spirit. The anointing is available to anyone who will dare to step out in faith for Jesus. So that means it's available for you! Every place you proclaim God's love, His presence will touch people's hearts.

How do you keep your lamp of passion, the calling of God on your life, burning strong? "Be dressed and ready for service. Keep your lamps burning" (Luke 12:35 NIV). You must constantly allow yourself to be consumed with God's vision to reach the entire world. Your obedience to seize every opportunity you have to share the love of God with others will keep that lamp burning strong in your heart.

When we no longer have vision for God's purposes, we will start doing things out of obligation. When we don't carefully guard our quality time with the Lord in our daily devotional then what we do for the Lord will be reduced to religious routine. That's a scary place to be because sometimes you don't even know you are in that place. To ensure that doesn't happen to you, I recommend you maintain a strong prayer life.

The more quality time you spend with God, the more you will identify with His heart for the lost. Your heart will be filled with His love and compassion. It will move you to see the hurting, the lost, and the broken in the way that Jesus sees them because you develop a heart for the people you pray for.

I spent a lot of time praying for my family before I ever attempted to share Christ with them. Many times I would be in tears as I prayed for them because I felt their pain and struggles. It's important to understand that we are not wrestling with flesh and blood but against spiritual forces of darkness. (Ephesians 6:12) The enemy wants to steal, kill and destroy. (John 10:10) Instead, we must withstand and defeat him with our spiritual weapons. (The ultimate weapons!) God has given us the blood of Jesus, the word of God, and the Holy Spirit.

So how do you keep a lamp burning? Mother Teresa, who became very popular for the work she did in reaching out to the poor and downtrodden in Calcutta put it very simply: "In order to keep a lamp burning, you have to keep putting oil in it."

You can have an oil lamp filled with oil until it overflows. But what good is an oil lamp filled with oil, if the fire has not been ignited?

Ask God to light up a fire in your heart, and keep that lamp burning through a lifestyle of obedience. A lamp that is not burning doesn't bring light to the darkness, although it has the necessary resources. It is not fulfilling the purpose for which it was created. Instead, it's just a lamp full of oil.

Your spiritual lamp is ignited through your obedience to the great commission. When you obey God as a minister of the gospel in sharing your faith, God's compassion will flood your heart, and it will move and compel you to action. Don't allow your heart to be desensitized to the cry of humanity all around you.

****

I remember the first day my son went to pre-school. My wife and I were excited, but because I was not used to the routine, I forgot to bring his lunch with him.

Hoping to correct my mistake, I spoke with my son's teacher.

"I'm sorry I forgot to bring his lunch box," I told her. "What time is lunch?"

"11:15," she said.

At 11:15 a.m., I returned to the school, lunchbox in hand. However when I returned, I discovered my son's class had already begun eating. For some reason, lunch had started early that day.

As I scanned the cafeteria, looking for my son, my eyes landed on a small, solitary figure sitting in the corner. It was Isaiah. Because he did not have his own food, he was sitting in the corner by himself.

I immediately strode over to where he was sitting, hugged him, apologized and handed him his lunch.

"How could the teacher allow this to happen?" I thought to myself, a bit emotional and teary eyed. As a parent, I never want my child to experience rejection; and I'd like to think that if I were his teacher, I would have found some way to prevent this child from feeling excluded from everyone else. I would have given him my own lunch to save him from feeling that way. However, as a father, I just spent time with him, trying to blot out his experience of rejection.

You see, that's the heart of our Heavenly Father, too. There are many people out there, outside of the four walls of the church, who feel rejected by society, their families, and loved ones. They feel rejection in a relationship and only the love of Jesus, the love of God, can bring healing and restoration into their lives.

But how can they receive it unless someone delivers it to them? How can they encounter God's unconditional love if we as God's people are too consumed with ourselves and have grown cold in our passion to reach out to them? Through your constant communion with God and simple acts of obedience, you will keep that lamp burning to be God's answer.

You have to keep that lamp burning. It's ignited through your obedience and cannot be ignited without obedience. There's no such thing as keeping the lamp burning that's never been lit. You have to get lit through action and through stepping out in faith. Otherwise, you're just on the shelf, a nice display of Christianity, but not being used for your intended purpose.

I want to burn brightly for the Lord. I want to be used for what I have been designed to do, and that is to burn brightly for the glory of God. Once that light has been lit, you need to keep putting oil in that lamp so it stays lit. This has to do with your direct communion with the Holy Spirit and the word of God. You've got to develop a strong dependence upon the Holy Spirit and remain constantly plugged into the Word. That's the only way to keep your lamp filled with oil (the anointing and the presence of God).

Maybe your oil lamp has gone empty or is dimly lit. What do you need to do? Spend time worshiping the Lord in singing, and praise Him for the wonderful works that He has done in your life. Learn to be still in prayer so that you can hear Him speak to your heart regarding His perfect will for you. Prayer is letting your request be known to God, but it is also listening to what He wants to speak into your heart. It begins with a simple act of obedience, a simple step of faith. It takes a simple prayer and priority adjustment to get that lamp burning strong once again.

Prayer:
"Lord, I humble myself in your presence. I ask you to forgive me for neglecting my responsibility to share Christ with others as a minister of the gospel. I pray, revive that fire and desire within me. Grant me boldness and flood my heart with your unconditional love for souls. Help me to discern the opportunities that you have given me to share my faith with others. I want to keep my lamp burning, Lord. I want to be deliberate, God, about my passionate pursuit in knowing you. I identify with the longing of Your heart to see the lost come to Jesus, to see the backslidden restored, to see the brokenhearted healed. I am a yielded vessel unto you from this day forward. I commit to take every opportunity that comes across my way. I'm going to seize it, by the power of your Holy Spirit. Here I am Lord, in the name of Jesus. Amen."

You can win multitudes to Christ, yet not make one disciple. Embrace the Great Commission in its entirety and not just partially.

Chapter 10

DISCIPLESHIP

And Jesus came and spoke to them, saying, "All authority has been given to Me in heaven and on earth. Go therefore and make disciples of all the nations, baptizing them in the name of the Father and of the Son and of the Holy Spirit, teaching them to observe all things that I have commanded you; and lo, I am with you always, even to the end of the age."
Matthew 28:18-20 NKJV

God has given me the wonderful privilege to be a part of a great team that is making a difference in the world. The Lord has blessed me with a beautiful wife and a son who loves God passionately. We love to serve in the ministry together at our local church here in Honolulu Hawaii.

I can honestly say that I am where I am today because someone believed in me from the very beginning. Pastor Art and Pastor Kuna Sepúlveda have spoken into our lives and helped us develop as disciples of Christ in our character, faith, love and integrity. Their leadership has inspired us to answer the call in fulfilling the great commission. It has all been made possible through Discipleship.

The great commission to me is two fold: First, we are to spread the good news of salvation to the world, that through Jesus we can all receive forgiveness of sin. Secondly, we are to make disciples in order to pass down God's vision for generations to come.

What does it mean to make disciples? It is about imparting and reproducing the heavenly mandate in the hearts of others so that they too can answer the call of God in their lives. We are to help mentor them in developing their character and faith.

If we are going to reach the world for Christ, it cannot be based on a few gifted individuals. Everyone who believes in Jesus as the Savior of the world must become a witness. The great commission was not just for the chosen few, but for all who would believe in Jesus. God's dream of reaching the multitudes is only possible when the local church not only focuses on evangelism, but discipleship as well.

I once visited a church and had fellowship with the assistant pastor. He took me on tour of their facilities, and I was absolutely amazed! Their sanctuary had the capacity to fit at least 20,000 people! They also had their own gymnasium, cafeteria, missions home, water baptism facility, and multiple classrooms! As a matter of fact, they owned the entire block.

I asked him, "How many church members do you currently have attending all the services combined?"

"We have a total of twenty five members," he replied.

I was shocked at his response. How could they own such a large piece of property and have so few members?

The pastor explained that there was a time when this church used to be filled to capacity on a weekly basis. Thousands of people would gather to hear the word of God. There was a hunger and thirst for God's presence in their lives. But the former Pastor had gotten old and eventually passed on to be with the Lord.

The ministry had been centered on one man, and once he was gone, the congregation began to dwindle. The past pastor had succeeded in reaching thousands of people, but he was unable to raise up another generation to carry the mantle after him.

As a minister of the gospel, we need to think about succession. Who will answer the call long after we are gone? I believe God desires for us to impact generations to come with the gospel of the Lord Jesus Christ. We must think generationally and not just in the here and now.

Jesus chose to commit Himself to disciple 12 men. He was always traveling from one city to the next, preaching about the kingdom of God. But there were only 12 who were constantly with Him everywhere He would travel. They ate with Him, traveled with Him, and ministered alongside Him. Throughout that time, Jesus began to mold their character and instill within them a spirit of conquest. He modeled the perfect example of what it meant to fulfill the Great Commission in its entirety.

"How God anointed Jesus of Nazareth with the Holy Spirit and with power, who went about doing good and

healing all who were oppressed by the devil, for God was with Him" (Acts 10:38 NKJV).

Throughout his human life, Jesus performed many miraculous signs. He healed the sick, cleansed the lepers and even raised the dead! He would rise up early in prayer and minister to the needs of the people throughout the day at every place He traveled.

In return, his disciples wrote about all they witnessed Jesus do, and they followed His example even after He ascended to the heavens. They willingly paid the price of spreading the good news even to the point of persecution.

What moved Jesus' disciples to such extremes? What compelled them to live their life for Christ? I believe it was done out of gratitude for God's unconditional love. The disciples personally witnessed Jesus pour out His life as a living sacrifice for the penalty of their sins; and for that, they were forever grateful.

We are to win souls and make disciples. Yet, as the empty church story illustrates, you can win multitudes to Christ, yet not make one disciple. Let's choose to embrace the heavenly mandate of reaching the world in its entirety.

Since you are reading this book, I believe you have a heart for the lost. You know there is so much more to life than the trappings of human existence: having a job, a career, a family, and so forth. You know you were called to change the world and to make a difference.

I want to encourage you to win the lost and be a disciple who makes other disciples. It's one thing for someone to answer the call to make a difference in their generation. It's an entirely different feat for a person to become a vessel who not only leads others to Christ, but also helps mobilize the church to win souls.

Let's help others answer the call to reach the world. Together, we can make an eternal difference from one generation to the next. We just need to follow the example that Jesus modeled for us in the gospels.

****

"Follow my example, as I follow the example of Christ" (1 Corinthians 11:1 NKJV).

The Apostle Paul wanted to emulate the example of Jesus. He traveled to many cities tirelessly proclaiming the gospel of Jesus Christ and made disciples at every place he visited. And he cared for his disciples as a father does his children.

Today, I have the wonderful privilege of discipling 12 men, who in turn are on a journey of each discipling 12 others. God has given us a divine strategy to win the world for Christ. It's not just about leading men to a Sinner's Prayer; it's about helping them to develop in character and faith so they can reach a place of spiritual maturity.

There are so many gifted young people who fall through the cracks because no one ever holds them accountable. The sad truth is that they do not have anyone speaking into their life.

No matter where we are and what we have achieved, in order to reach our potential, we need someone to disciple us.

Many are quick to step up and lead others without being a disciple themselves. My advice is to always take upon the heart of a humble student. Discipleship is not just encouragement; it's also correction in areas of our lives when needed. I believe that through discipleship, we can multiply the shepherd's care to reach the multitude and bring each believer to a place of maturity where they are strong in their faith and solid in character.

It is so rewarding to see ordinary men and women become the mighty vessels of God they were destined to be. They realize that they are not in this world merely to have a good time. Instead, they have a divine purpose and calling to be a mouthpiece for the Lord.

The amazing thing about all of this is that God empowers His people to carry out such a great undertaking. In all that you do for the Lord, never forget it is His love for us that compels us to reach others. Now is our time to compel them to come in so that the house of the Lord may be filled. God is not willing that any should perish, but that all would come to a personal relationship with Jesus Christ.

I would like to share a testimony about one of the men I have decided to disciple. Discipleship has made an impact in his spiritual growth because of the fact that he allowed someone to speak into his life. He has only been with me for a short time yet I have seen him grow in his faith, character and leadership.

Mikes' Testimony

I used to be all kinds of messed up as I am sure many of us are in our own way. I was doing things from adultery, lying, manipulating people, pornography, gossiping about others, and the list goes on. What I didn't realize was that God had a plan for my life. That was one of the first things I learned, and it shook my world. I had been in and out of church throughout my whole life. The thing is, I still had no real relationship with Christ. It still wasn't until I hit rock bottom that I truly had my own encounter with God and realized I couldn't do anything without Him. By His grace, I came under the leadership of Pastor Wally to become one of his Disciples, and that's truly when my life transformed from a Christian man to a Disciple for Christ Jesus. Pastor Wally has shown me that being a Disciple is not about the works we do for God, but about having a heart for people and the love for God and all He has done for us. I am not perfect, but in the eyes of my Father I was made perfect and His will on my life no man can change. Discipleship is about growing your connection with Jesus, about learning to listen to the Holy Spirit, allowing God to use you the way He always intended. I no longer practice religion; I AM a Disciple for Christ. I have not yet arrived and I still have much to learn and grow, but living a Disciple's life has allowed me to see God's grace and love for not only my life but the lives of others around me. So the question that I ask my own Disciples is, "What are you doing to ensure your family, your friends and those around you will inherit eternal life in Heaven? Pastor Art Sepulveda said "Have you ever imagined what God can do in your city using you as His instrument?" I never used to, but now as His Disciple I imagine it all the time.

I pray that the teachings contained in this book have awakened a sense of purpose within you. God loves to show Himself strong on the behalf of those whose hearts are loyal to Him. Welcome to the new breed of believers that God is raising up in this generation. Together, let's compel them to come in that the house of the Lord may be filled. God's mighty hand is upon you.

Prayer:

"Father, I commit to be a fully devoted follower of Christ. Help me to be the disciple you have called me to be: a person of faith and character who is compelled by your unconditional love to make a difference in this world. I declare that I am bold as a lion, and I will not fear. A spark has been ignited within my heart, and I intend to keep that passion burning for the Lord all the days of my life. Every step of faith I take will unfold your master plan. Flood my heart with your compassion at all times. I pray that I would see as Jesus saw. I believe that there is an urgency within me more than ever before to reach out to a lost and dying world. Enlarge my heart for humanity God, more and more. I answer the call upon my life to be a minister of the gospel. I believe that your mighty hand of protection is upon me Lord. In Jesus' name I pray. Amen."

NOTES

Chapter 1: Compel
Michael & Carol Hart
"Reaching Every Person. Rescuing Every Child." www.gozoe.org

Chapter 2: Bold as a Lion
Madagascar 2005 Movie, Animation
https://en.wikipedia.org/wiki/Tondo,_Manila

Chapter 3: Master Plan
The Touch of the Master's Hand https://en.wikipedia.org/wiki/
The_Touch_of_theM_aster's_Hand

Chapter 4: Compassion
Chinese toddler struck by 2 trucks
https://www.youtube.com/watch?v=N9KuUR2-p9Q

Chapter 5: Spark

Chapter 6: Hunger

Chapter 7: Urgency

Chapter 8: Enlarge My Heart

Chapter 9: Keep Your Lamp Burning
Mother Teresa
"To keep a lamp burning, we have to keep putting oil in it."
http://www.brainyquote.com/quotes/quotes/m/
mothertere132068.html

Chapter 10: Discipleship

COMPEL

For more information about the author
please visit us online at
www.compel.life

www.ingramcontent.com/pod-product-compliance
Lightning Source LLC
Chambersburg PA
CBHW072013040426

42447CB00009B/1613